To Gr, ♡
From San Antonio, Texas
Love,
Daddy

EUROPE

ASIA

AFRICA

AUSTRALASIA

ANTARCTICA

Authors and Illustrators:

Wonderful World	Fun Facts	Amazing Animals
Angela Royston	Andy Charman	Jenny Vaughan
and Gerald Hawksley	and Gillian Clements	and Ann Savage

This edition first published in 1997 by
SMITHMARK Publishers Inc.
a division of U.S. Media Holdings Inc.,
115 West 18th Street, New York, NY 10011

SMITHMARK books are available for bulk purchase for
sales promotion and premium use. For details write or call
the manager of special sales, SMITHMARK Publishers,
115 West 18th Street, New York, NY 10011

Produced by Anness Publishing Limited
Hermes House, 88-89 Blackfriars Road
London SE1 8HA

ISBN 0-7651-9406-6

Publisher Joanna Lorenz
Editorial Consultant Jackie Fortey
Senior Editor Belinda Wilkinson
Project Editor Isabel Clark
Designers Joy Fitzsimmons, Marilyn Clay, Nigel Soper

Thanks to Isabel Clark and Educational Advisor Jonathan R Allen

Printed in Singapore by Star Standard Industries Pte. Ltd.

1 0 9 8 7 6 5 4 3 2

My
First Book
of
KNOWLEDGE

SMITHMARK

CONTENTS

WONDERFUL WORLD

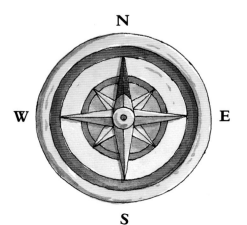

CONTENTS

FUN FACTS

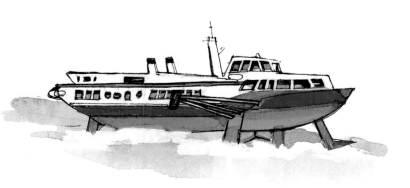

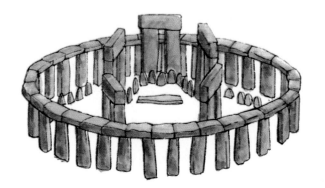

CONTENTS

AMAZING ANIMALS

Wonderful
WORLD

Equator

THE EARTH IN SPACE

The Earth is one of nine planets that spin around the hot Sun. The Moon spins around the Earth. The Sun is millions of miles away but it gives us light and heat.

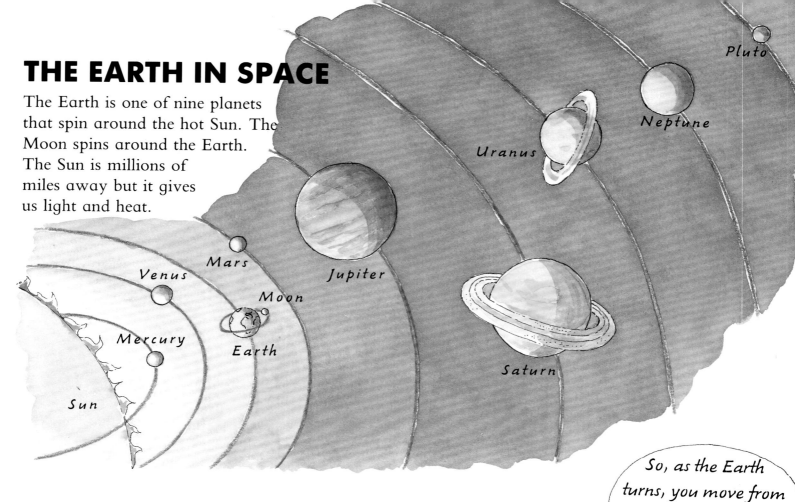

NIGHT AND DAY

The Earth is like a spinning top with the North Pole at the top and the South Pole at the bottom. Each spin takes 24 hours and, at any time, half the Earth is in daylight while the other half is in darkness.

So, as the Earth turns, you move from day into night and back into day again.

When the southern half of the globe leans towards the Sun, the north is darker and colder – it is winter.

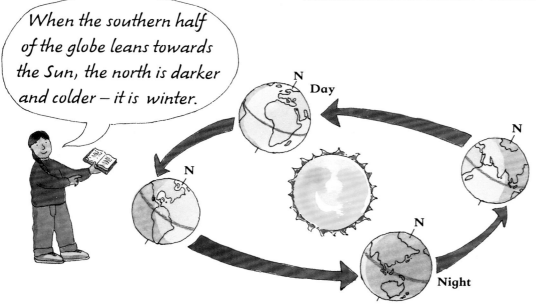

THE SEASONS

The Earth takes one year to orbit the Sun. The Equator is an imaginary line around the middle of the Earth. The Sun always shines strongly here and it is always hot. The Earth, however, is tilted. When the southern half leans towards the Sun, the days there are longer and hotter. It is summer.

WHAT IS A MAP?

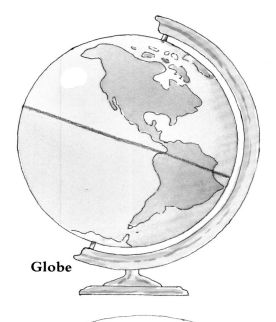

Globe

The most accurate way to show the land and the oceans is to make a round model of the Earth, called a globe. Then you can see where each country is and how big it is.

Most maps show flat pictures of the Earth. But how do map-makers turn a round ball into a flat rectangle? They either cut zigzags around the North and South Poles or they stretch the land there to fill the gaps.

Try it yourself next time you peel an orange. Keep the peel in one piece and lay it flat.

Some maps look like peeled orange skin.

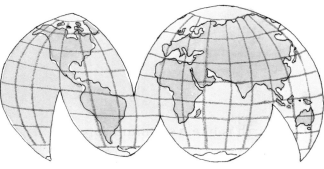

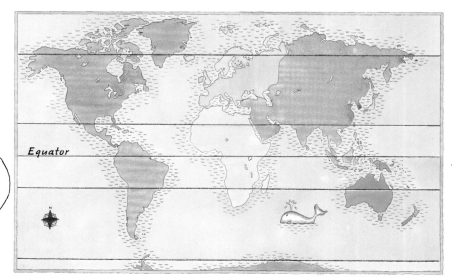

Equator

Look for these other imaginary lines on the maps in the book.

The Equator is an imaginary line around the Earth.

COMPASS ROSE

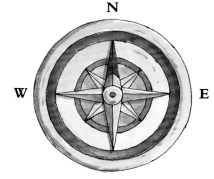

N

W   E

S

Maps are always drawn with north at the top and south at the bottom. This means that east is always on the right and west on the left. The compass rose on each map shows exactly where north is.

11

HOW TO READ THE MAPS

If you floated over the Earth in a balloon, the land below would change from farmland to mountains, deserts, forests and ice. Sometimes you would float over big cities, sometimes over lakes and rivers. The higher you were, the bigger the area you would see at once. Look at our maps to find out what kind of landscape you would see.

Desert

Mountains

Tropical rainforest

Grassland or prairie

Woodland and farmland

Pine forest

Tundra and ice

If you were in a balloon, you would not know where you were unless you had a map. Only the map tells you the names of the countries, rivers, mountains and cities. It shows the borders between different countries. Look for these symbols and names on each map:

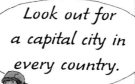
Look out for a capital city in every country.

Capital city

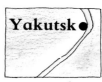
Large city

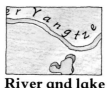
Country border

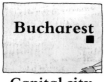
State border

River and lake

Sea or ocean

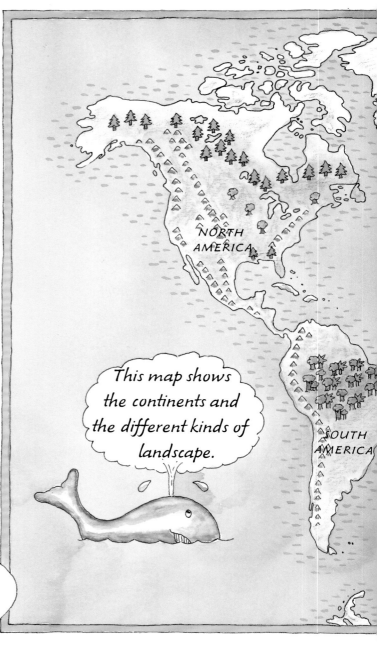
This map shows the continents and the different kinds of landscape.

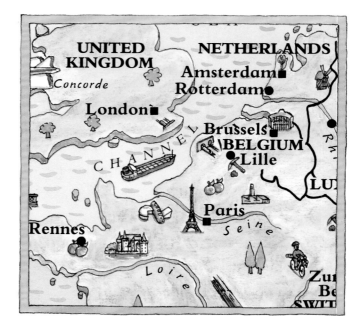

12

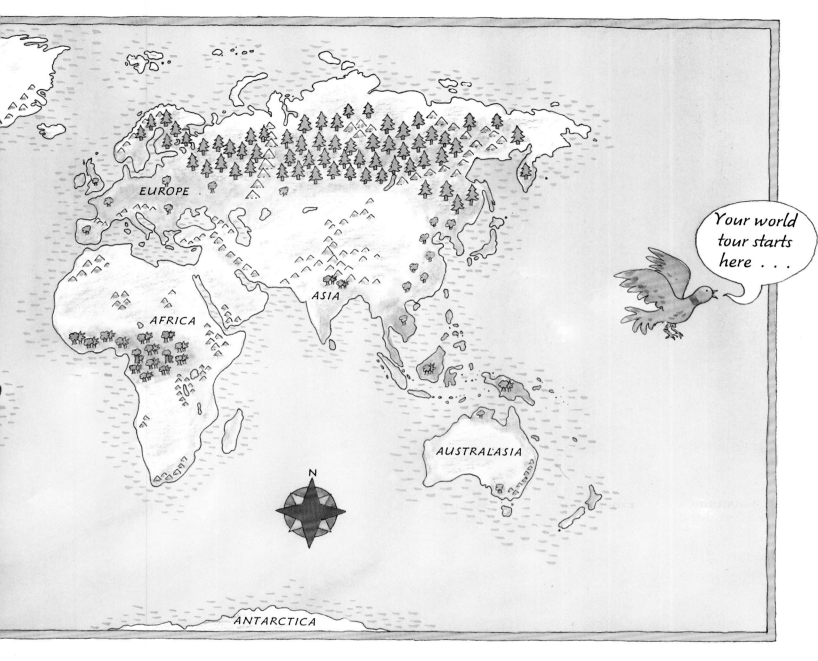

EUROPE

ASIA

AFRICA

AUSTRALASIA

Your world tour starts here . . .

ANTARCTICA

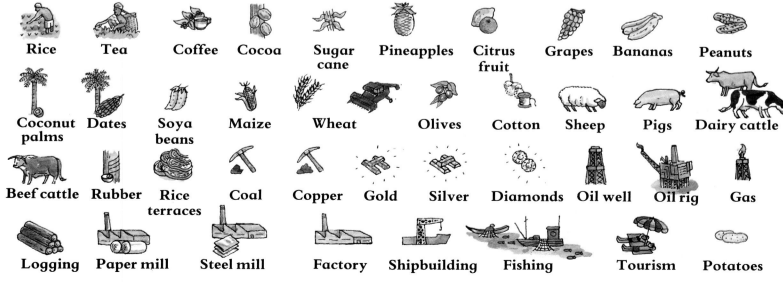

Rice **Tea** **Coffee** **Cocoa** **Sugar cane** **Pineapples** **Citrus fruit** **Grapes** **Bananas** **Peanuts**

Coconut palms **Dates** **Soya beans** **Maize** **Wheat** **Olives** **Cotton** **Sheep** **Pigs** **Dairy cattle**

Beef cattle **Rubber** **Rice terraces** **Coal** **Copper** **Gold** **Silver** **Diamonds** **Oil well** **Oil rig** **Gas**

Logging **Paper mill** **Steel mill** **Factory** **Shipbuilding** **Fishing** **Tourism** **Potatoes**

Here are some of the pictures you will see on many of the maps.

CANADA and Alaska

Canada is the second largest country in the world. It stretches from the Rocky Mountains in the west to the Atlantic Ocean. The land in the far north is always covered with snow. Many wild animals live here and in the forests. Most of the people live in the south, and work in the big cities, near the border with the United States of America.

Can you see?

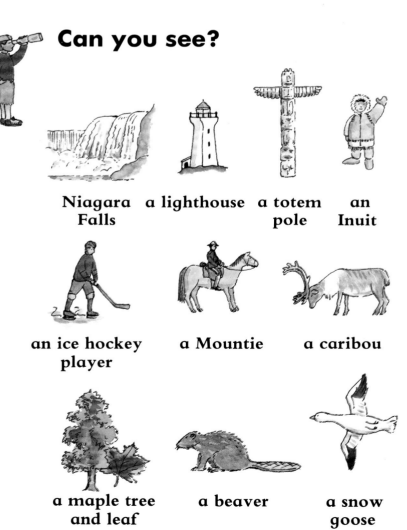

Niagara Falls **a lighthouse** **a totem pole** **an Inuit**

an ice hockey player **a Mountie** **a caribou**

a maple tree and leaf **a beaver** **a snow goose**

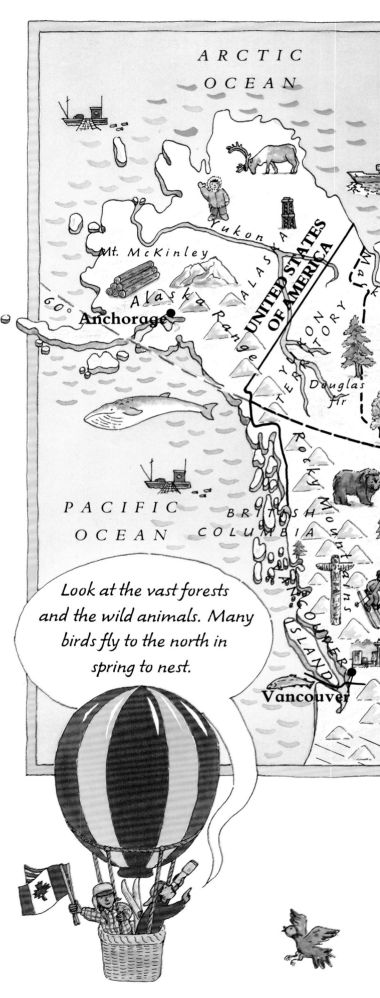

ARCTIC OCEAN

Mt. McKinley

Anchorage

Yukon

ALASKA

UNITED STATES OF AMERICA

YUKON TERRITORY

Mackenzie

Alaska Range

Douglas fir

60°

PACIFIC OCEAN

BRITISH COLUMBIA

Rocky Mountains

VANCOUVER ISLAND

Look at the vast forests and the wild animals. Many birds fly to the north in spring to nest.

Vancouver

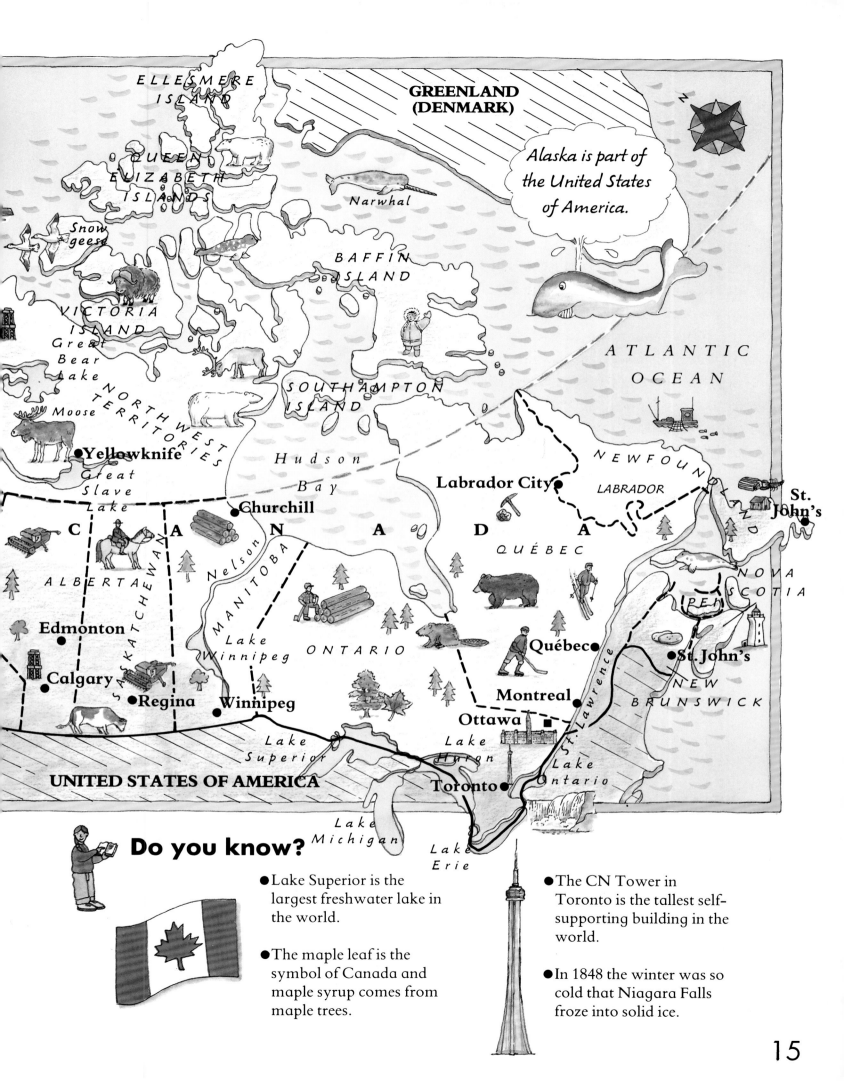

ELLESMERE ISLAND

GREENLAND (DENMARK)

QUEEN ELIZABETH ISLANDS

Snow geese

Narwhal

BAFFIN ISLAND

Alaska is part of the United States of America.

ATLANTIC OCEAN

VICTORIA ISLAND

Great Bear Lake

SOUTHAMPTON ISLAND

NORTHWEST TERRITORIES

Moose

Yellowknife

Great Slave Lake

Hudson Bay

Labrador City

NEWFOUN

LABRADOR

St. John's

C   A

Churchill

N   A

D   A

QUÉBEC

Nelson

ALBERTA

MANITOBA

ONTARIO

Lake Winnipeg

NOVA SCOTIA

P.E.I.

Edmonton

SASKATCHEWAN

Québec

St. John's

Calgary

NEW BRUNSWICK

Regina

Winnipeg

Montreal

St. Lawrence

Ottawa

Lake Superior

Lake Huron

Lake Ontario

UNITED STATES OF AMERICA

Lake Michigan

Toronto

Lake Erie

Do you know?

- Lake Superior is the largest freshwater lake in the world.

- The maple leaf is the symbol of Canada and maple syrup comes from maple trees.

- The CN Tower in Toronto is the tallest self-supporting building in the world.

- In 1848 the winter was so cold that Niagara Falls froze into solid ice.

UNITED STATES OF AMERICA

Native American Indians were the first people to live in this huge country. Now people from all over the world live here too. Most people work in factories and offices in big cities. There are many farms, including huge cattle ranches and wheat farms on the prairies. There is still plenty of space for wild animals in the mountains, deserts, forests and rivers.

Can you see?

The Golden Gate Bridge

The Capitol

The Statue of Liberty

a Pueblo Indian pot

a Mississippi steamboat

an American football player

a jazz singer

The Grand Canyon

a dinosaur fossil

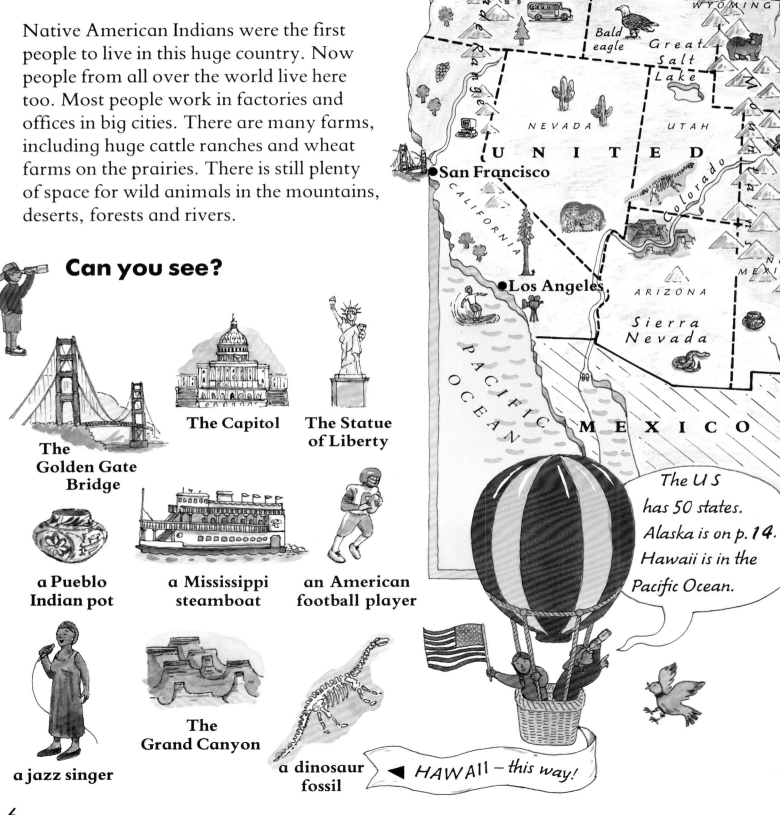

The US has 50 states. Alaska is on p. 14. Hawaii is in the Pacific Ocean.

◄ HAWAII – this way!

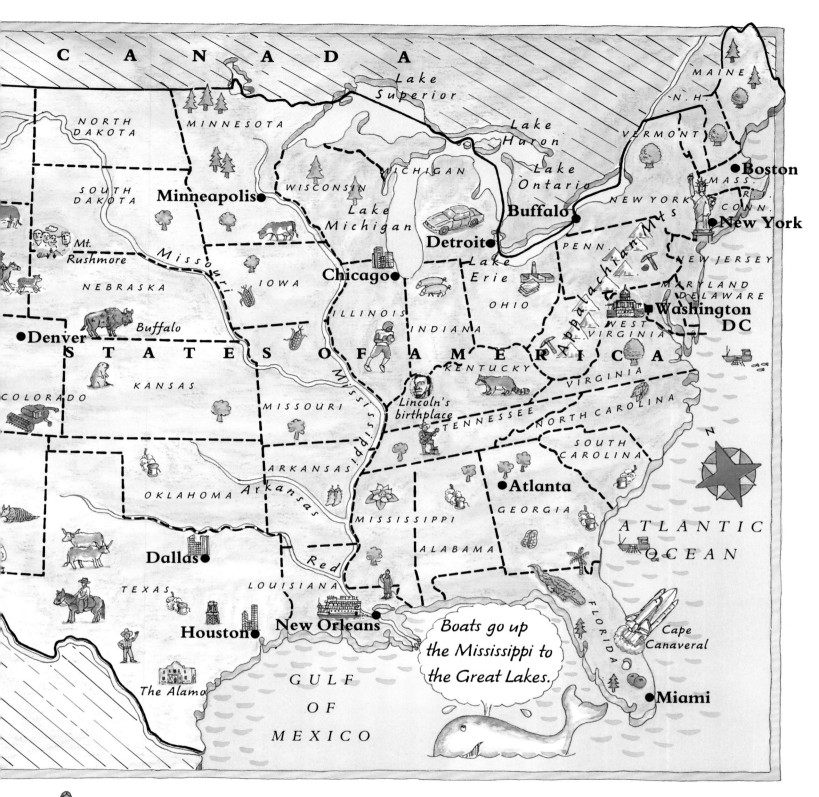

Boats go up the Mississippi to the Great Lakes.

Do you know?

- The heads of 4 great American presidents are carved into Mount Rushmore.

- A giant sequoia is the most massive tree in the world. It can grow as tall as a 28-story building.

- Potato chips were invented by a Native American called George Crumm.

CENTRAL AMERICA

Central America is a bridge of land between North and South America. Thick rainforest covers the sides of the mountains. Most people are farmers. They grow coffee, sugar and fruit.

Tropical fruits, sugar and spices also grow well on the beautiful islands of the Caribbean. Tourists come here to enjoy the hot sunshine, the sea and the happy Caribbean music.

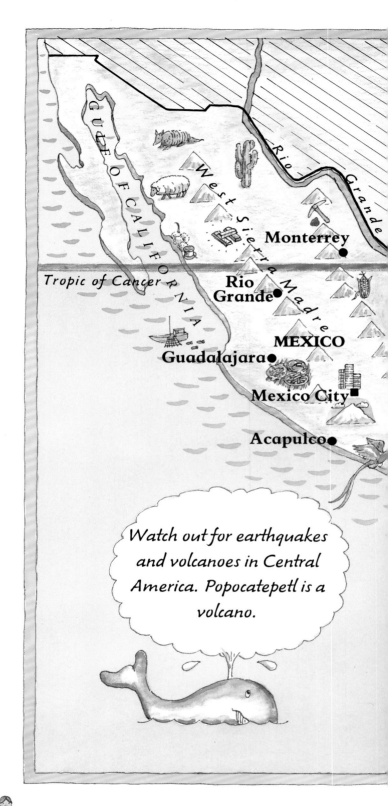

Watch out for earthquakes and volcanoes in Central America. Popocatepetl is a volcano.

Can you see?

Popocatepetl

an ancient Mayan city

Panama Canal

Mexican folk dancers

a steel band

a cricket player

a coral reef

a scuba diver

a quetzal

an armadillo

Do you know?

● Mexico City is the largest city in the world. More people live here than in the whole of Australia.

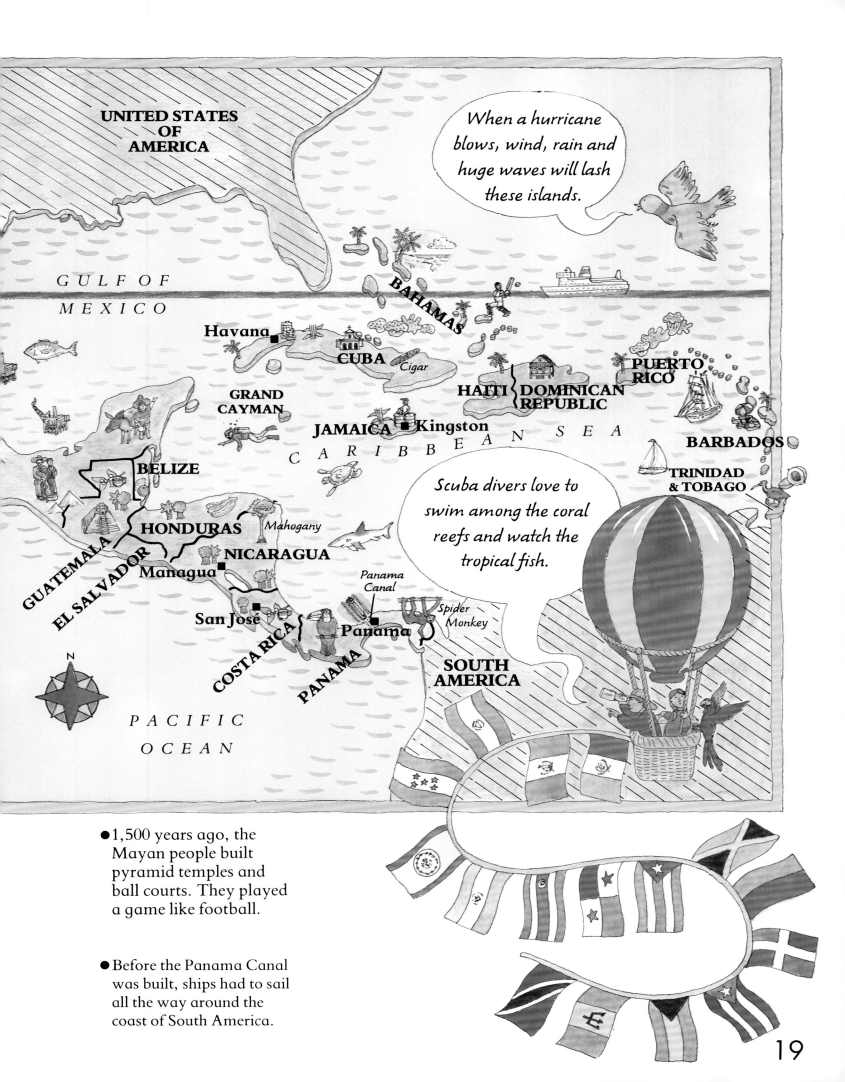

UNITED STATES
OF
AMERICA

GULF OF
MEXICO

When a hurricane blows, wind, rain and huge waves will lash these islands.

BAHAMAS

Havana
CUBA   Cigar

GRAND
CAYMAN

JAMAICA   ■ Kingston

HAITI   DOMINICAN
         REPUBLIC

PUERTO
RICO

C A R I B B E A N   S E A

BARBADOS

BELIZE

Mahogany

TRINIDAD
& TOBAGO

HONDURAS

NICARAGUA

Managua ■

GUATEMALA

EL SALVADOR

San José

COSTA RICA

Panama Canal

Panama

PANAMA

Spider
Monkey

Scuba divers love to swim among the coral reefs and watch the tropical fish.

SOUTH
AMERICA

PACIFIC
OCEAN

N

● 1,500 years ago, the Mayan people built pyramid temples and ball courts. They played a game like football.

● Before the Panama Canal was built, ships had to sail all the way around the coast of South America.

19

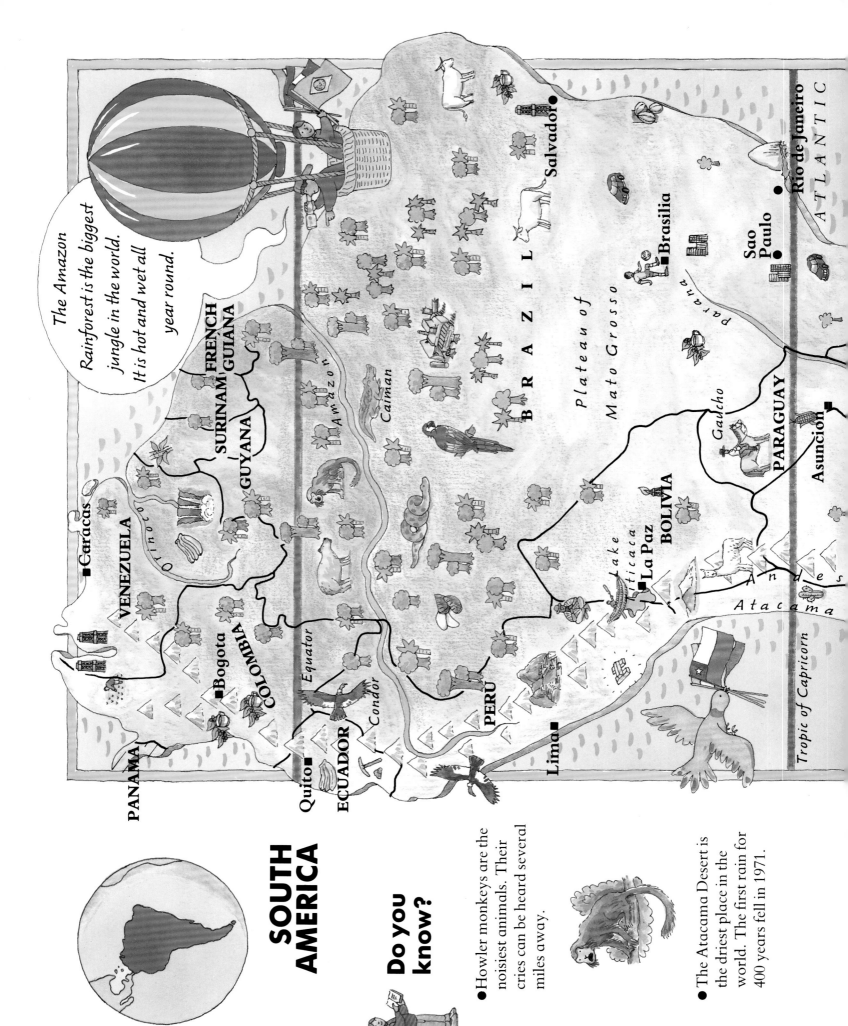

SOUTH AMERICA

The Amazon Rainforest is the biggest jungle in the world. It is hot and wet all year round.

Do you know?

- Howler monkeys are the noisiest animals. Their cries can be heard several miles away.

- The Atacama Desert is the driest place in the world. The first rain for 400 years fell in 1971.

PANAMA

VENEZUELA

■Caracas

COLOMBIA

■Bogota

Orinoco

FRENCH GUIANA

SURINAM

GUYANA

ECUADOR

Quito■

Equator

Condor

Amazon

Caiman

B R A Z I L

■Salvador

Plateau of Mato Grosso

■Brasilia

Parana

Sao Paulo

Rio de Janeiro

A T L A N T I C

PERU

Lima■

Lake Titicaca

La Paz■

BOLIVIA

Gaucho

PARAGUAY

Asuncion■

A n d e s

Atacama

Tropic of Capricorn

20

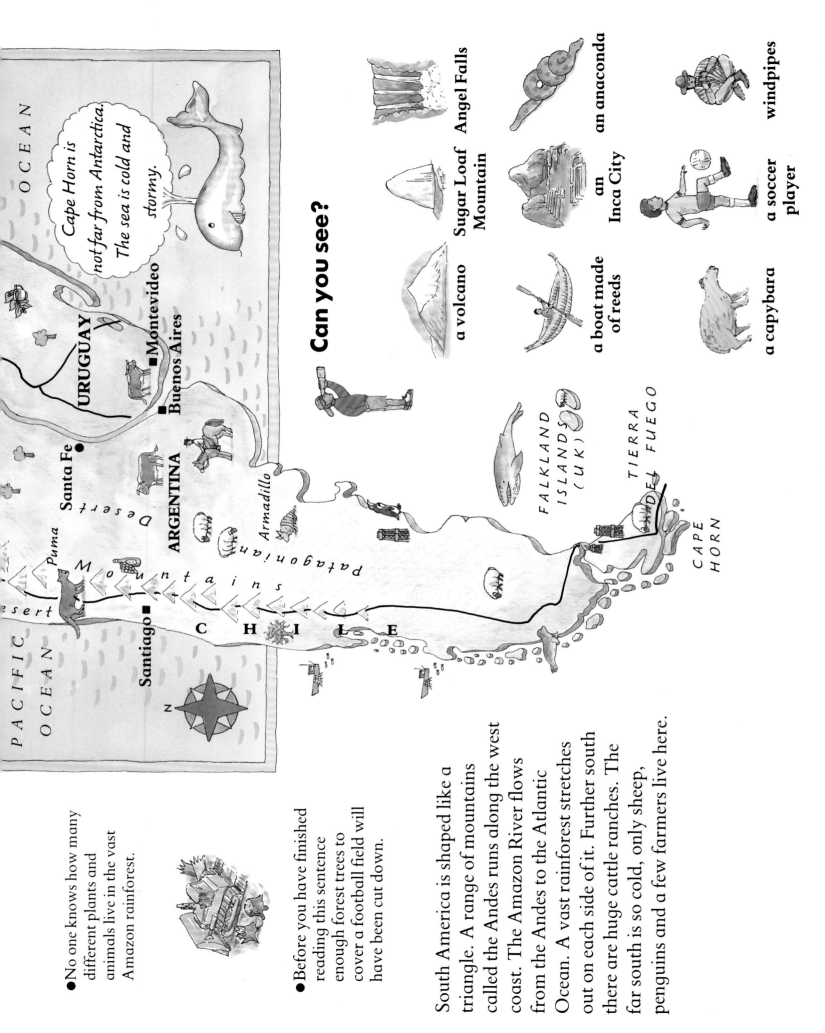

Cape Horn is not far from Antarctica. The sea is cold and stormy.

OCEAN

PACIFIC OCEAN

URUGUAY

■Montevideo

Buenos Aires

Santa Fe ●

Puma

Desert

ARGENTINA

M o u n t a i n s

Patagonian

Desert

Santiago ■

C H I L E

Armadillo

N

FALKLAND ISLANDS (UK)

TIERRA DEL FUEGO

CAPE HORN

Can you see?

a volcano

Sugar Loaf Mountain

Angel Falls

a boat made of reeds

an Inca City

an anaconda

a capybara

a soccer player

windpipes

● No one knows how many different plants and animals live in the vast Amazon rainforest.

● Before you have finished reading this sentence enough forest trees to cover a football field will have been cut down.

South America is shaped like a triangle. A range of mountains called the Andes runs along the west coast. The Amazon River flows from the Andes to the Atlantic Ocean. A vast rainforest stretches out on each side of it. Further south there are huge cattle ranches. The far south is so cold, only sheep, penguins and a few farmers live here.

WESTERN EUROPE

Much of the land in Western Europe is used for farming, but most people live in towns and cities. Many cities are hundreds of years old. People come from all over the world to see the historic buildings. The countries around the Mediterranean are hot and sunny in summer. Then the beaches are crowded with sunbathers, windsurfers and sailboats.

Can you see?

The Colosseum

a gondolier

The Eiffel Tower

a Flamenco dancer

a windmill

Channel Tunnel

a castle on the Loire

Leaning Tower of Pisa

Mount Etna

22

NORTH SEA

DENMARK

Hamburg

Berlin

POLAND

●Dublin

UNITED KINGDOM

Concorde

NETHERLANDS

Amsterdam

Rotterdam

London

Brussels

BELGIUM

Lille

Cologne

Bonn

Brandenburg Gate

GERMANY

CZECH REPUBLIC

SLOVAKIA

Rhine

LUX

ENGLISH CHANNEL

Paris

Seine

Vienna

Rennes

Loire

Munich

Danube

AUSTRIA

HUNGARY

Zurich

Bern

SWITZERLAND

Geneva

Lake Geneva

SLOVENIA

FRANCE

Venice

Bordeaux

Garonne

Lyons

Turin

Milan

BOSNIA-HERZEGOVINA

ALPS

APENNINES

ADRIATIC SEA

Bilbao

Ibex

Pyrenees

Wild boar

Florence

MONACO

Marseille

CORSICA

Rome

Ebro

SPAIN

ANDORRA

Barcelona

Po

Olive tree

Madrid

Naples●

ITALY

Pizza

Tagus

MALLORCA

SARDINIA

Paella

The Alhambra

MEDITERRANEAN SEA

SICILY

Mt. Etna

●Seville

Rock of Gibraltar

GIBRALTAR

MALTA

Do you know?

- For nearly 50 years Germany was divided into two countries.

- The Vatican in Rome is the smallest country in the world. The Pope lives there.

- The French TGV is the fastest passenger train. It is twice as fast as an ordinary train.

- The St Gotthard tunnel is the longest road tunnel in the world. It goes right under the Alps.

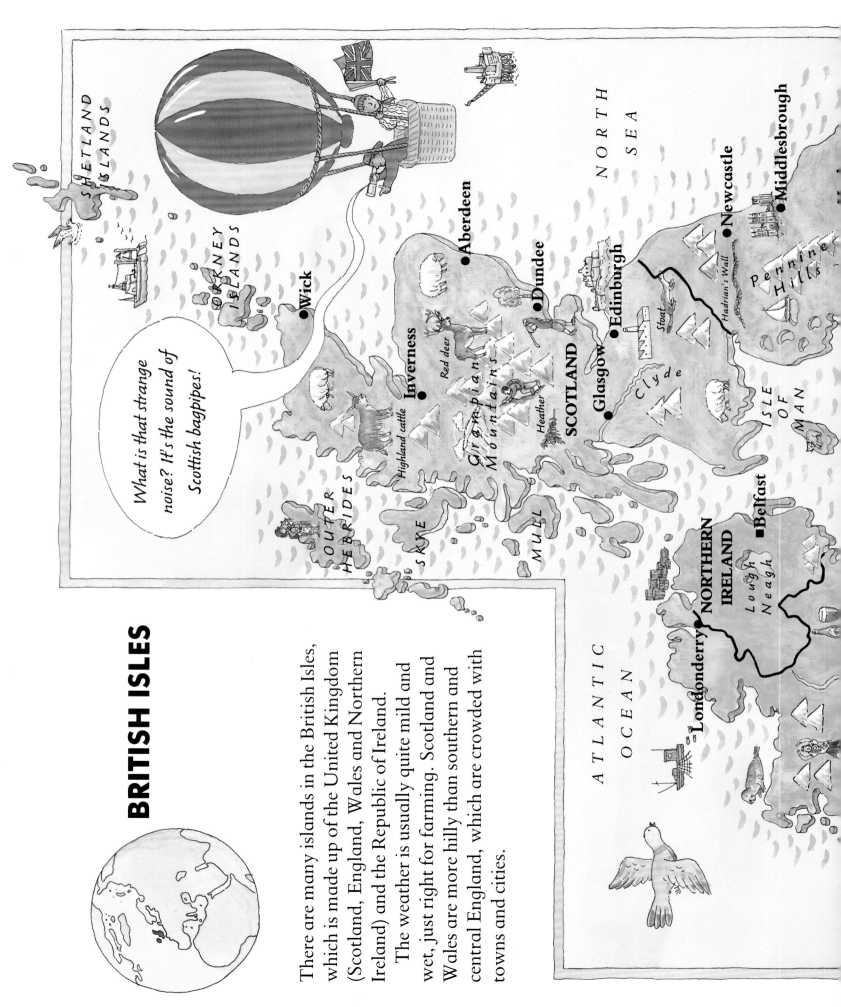

BRITISH ISLES

There are many islands in the British Isles, which is made up of the United Kingdom (Scotland, England, Wales and Northern Ireland) and the Republic of Ireland.

The weather is usually quite mild and wet, just right for farming. Scotland and Wales are more hilly than southern and central England, which are crowded with towns and cities.

What is that strange noise? It's the sound of Scottish bagpipes!

SHETLAND ISLANDS

ORKNEY ISLANDS

Wick

OUTER HEBRIDES

SKYE

MULL

Inverness

Red deer

Highland cattle

Grampian Mountains

Heather

Aberdeen

Dundee

SCOTLAND

Edinburgh

Glasgow

Clyde

Stoat

Hadrian's Wall

Pennine Hills

Newcastle

Middlesbrough

NORTH SEA

ISLE OF MAN

NORTHERN IRELAND

Belfast

Lough Neagh

Londonderry

ATLANTIC OCEAN

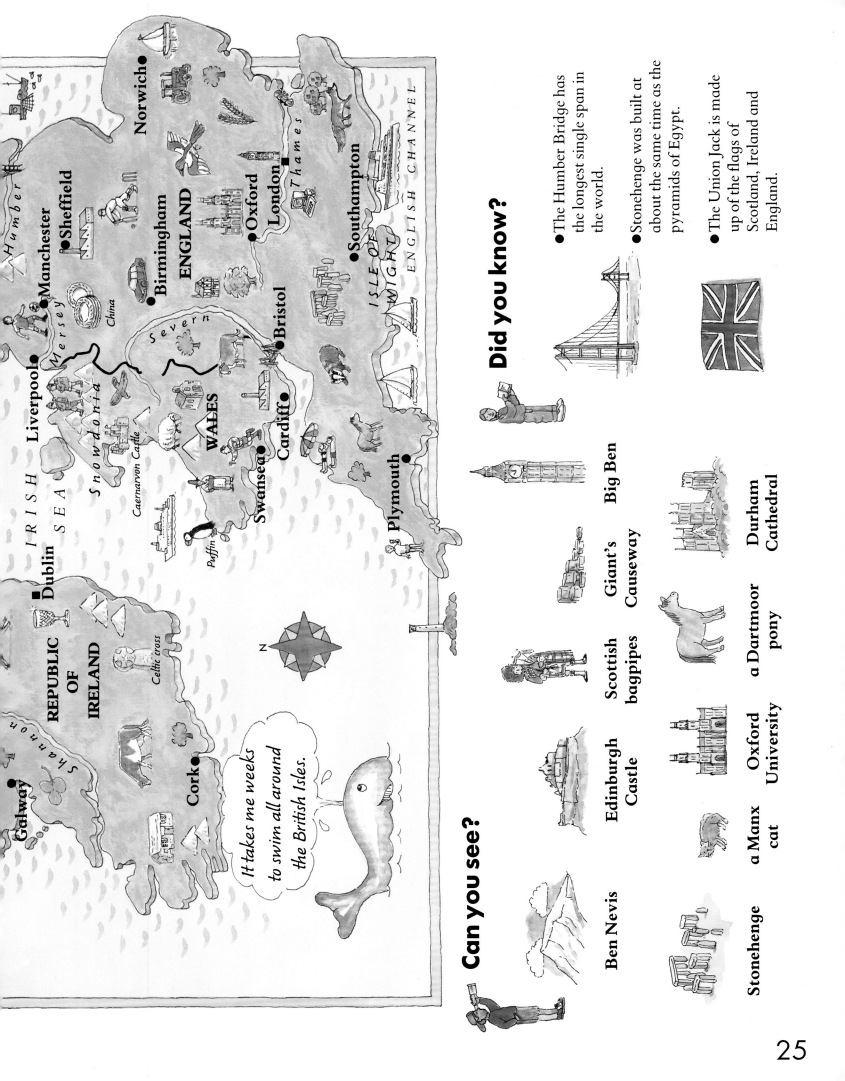

ENGLAND

Norwich
Sheffield
Manchester
Birmingham
Oxford
London
Southampton
ISLE OF WIGHT
Liverpool
Bristol
Cardiff
Swansea
Plymouth
WALES
Snowdonia
Caernarvon Castle
Mersey
Humber
China
Severn
Thames
IRISH SEA
ENGLISH CHANNEL
Puffin

REPUBLIC OF IRELAND
Dublin
Galway
Cork
Shannon
Celtic cross

It takes me weeks to swim all around the British Isles.

N

Can you see?

Ben Nevis

a Manx cat
Oxford University

Edinburgh Castle
Scottish bagpipes
a Dartmoor pony

Giant's Causeway
Big Ben
Durham Cathedral

Stonehenge

Did you know?

- The Humber Bridge has the longest single span in the world.
- Stonehenge was built at about the same time as the pyramids of Egypt.
- The Union Jack is made up of the flags of Scotland, Ireland and England.

25

EASTERN EUROPE

Most of Eastern Europe is covered with rugged mountains and forests. Only Poland and the land around the great Danube River is flat. Farmers here grow grapes, potatoes and other crops. They keep pigs, geese and cows. Barges and ships carry goods through Eastern Europe along the Danube. Winter is cold and snowy in the north, but the south is much warmer.

Can you see?

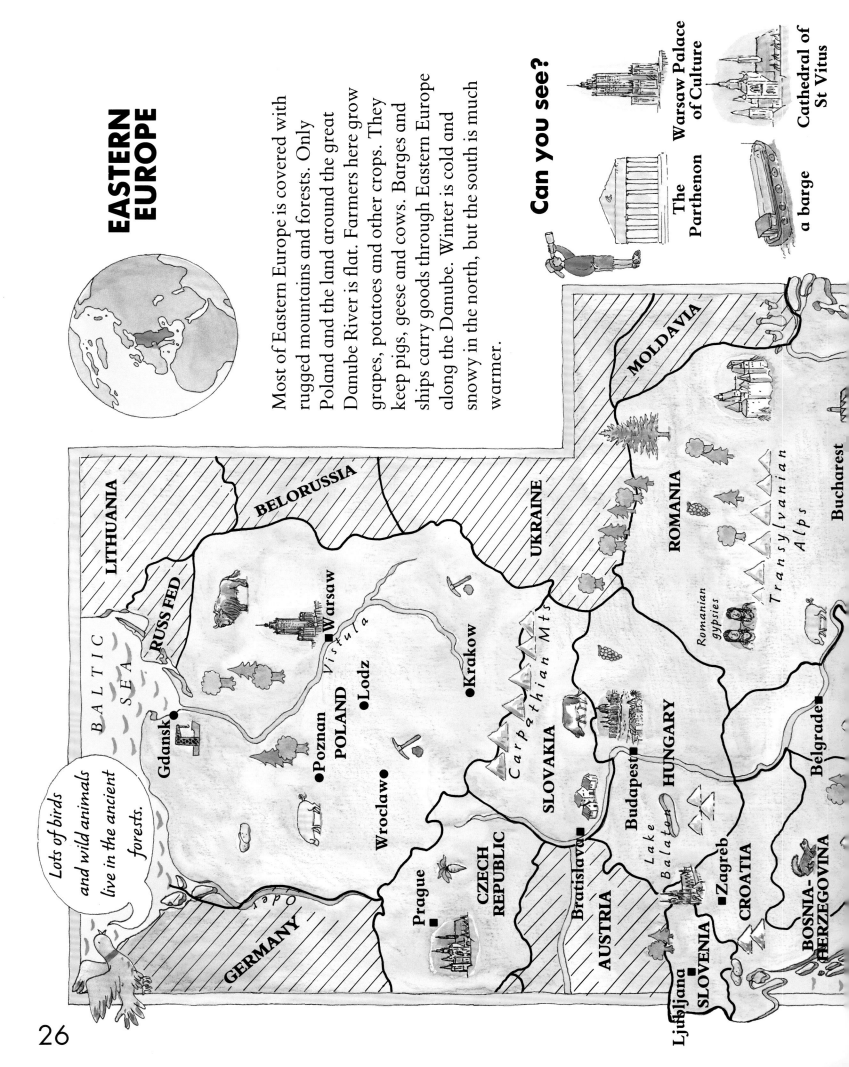

Warsaw Palace of Culture

Cathedral of St Vitus

The Parthenon

a barge

Lots of birds and wild animals live in the ancient forests.

GERMANY

BALTIC SEA

Gdansk

RUSS FED

LITHUANIA

BELORUSSIA

Poznan

POLAND

Warsaw

Vistula

Lodz

Wroclaw

Krakow

Odra

Prague

CZECH REPUBLIC

AUSTRIA

Bratislava

SLOVAKIA

Carpathian Mts

UKRAINE

Budapest

HUNGARY

Lake Balaton

Ljubljana

SLOVENIA

Zagreb

CROATIA

BOSNIA-HERZEGOVINA

Belgrade

MOLDAVIA

ROMANIA

Romanian gypsies

Transylvanian Alps

Bucharest

folk dancers

Bran Castle

a bison

gypsies

a polecat

an octopus

Do you know?

- The first Olympic games were held over 2,000 years ago in Olympia, Greece.

- A canal joins the River Danube to the Rhine. Ships can sail from the North Sea to the Black Sea.

- The story of the famous vampire, Count Dracula, is set in the mountains of Transylvania.

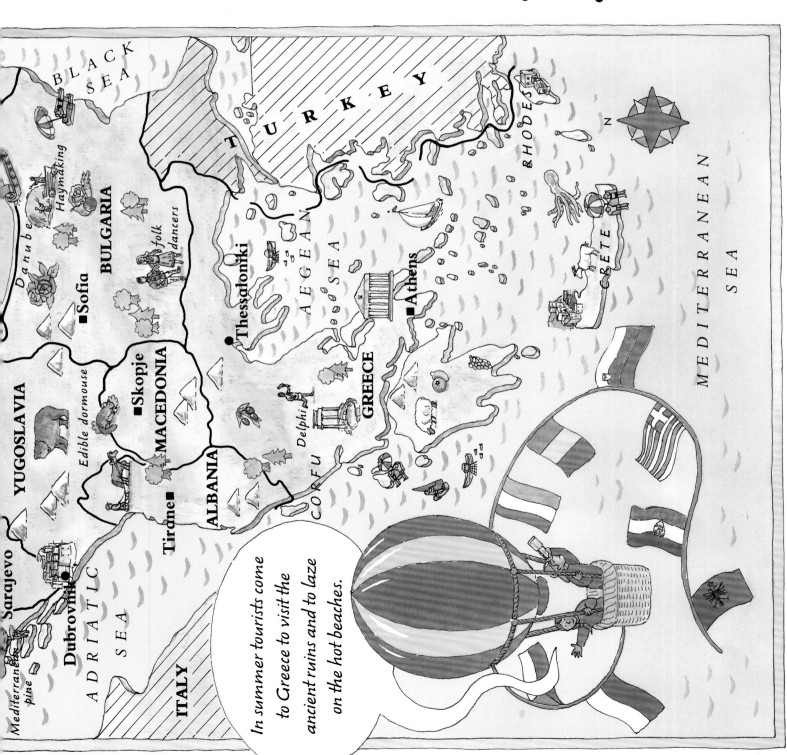

BLACK SEA

TURKEY

Haymaking

Danube

BULGARIA

roses

■Sofia

folk dancers

RHODES

●Thessaloniki

AEGEAN SEA

CRETE

YUGOSLAVIA

Edible dormouse

■Skopje

MACEDONIA

■Athens

Sarajevo

Dubrovnik●

Tirane■

ALBANIA

GREECE

Delphi

CORFU

Mediterranean pine

ADRIATIC SEA

ITALY

MEDITERRANEAN SEA

N

In summer tourists come to Greece to visit the ancient ruins and to laze on the hot beaches.

NORTHERN EUROPE

ICELAND

■**Reykjavik**

Does Santa Claus really live in Lapland? Look, those Laplanders are using reindeer to pull their sled.

Lakes and forests cover much of Northern Europe. The winters here are very cold, and people often use skis or sleds, as well as cars. Some of the trees are cut down to make timber and paper. Most people live in cities and on farms in the south. Many Norwegians work at sea, in fishing trawlers or on oil rigs.

Can you see?

Lego village

a Laplander

a cross-country skier

a lemming

a flying squirrel

a paper mill

a fishing trawler

a Viking ship

a fjord

Do you know?

● Hans Christian Andersen is Denmark's most famous writer. There is a bronze statue of his Little Mermaid in Copenhagen harbour.

● Hot water from Iceland's geysers provides central heating to the homes of Reykjavik.

● Lapland (in the far north) is called the Land of the Midnight Sun because it is light all night in summer.

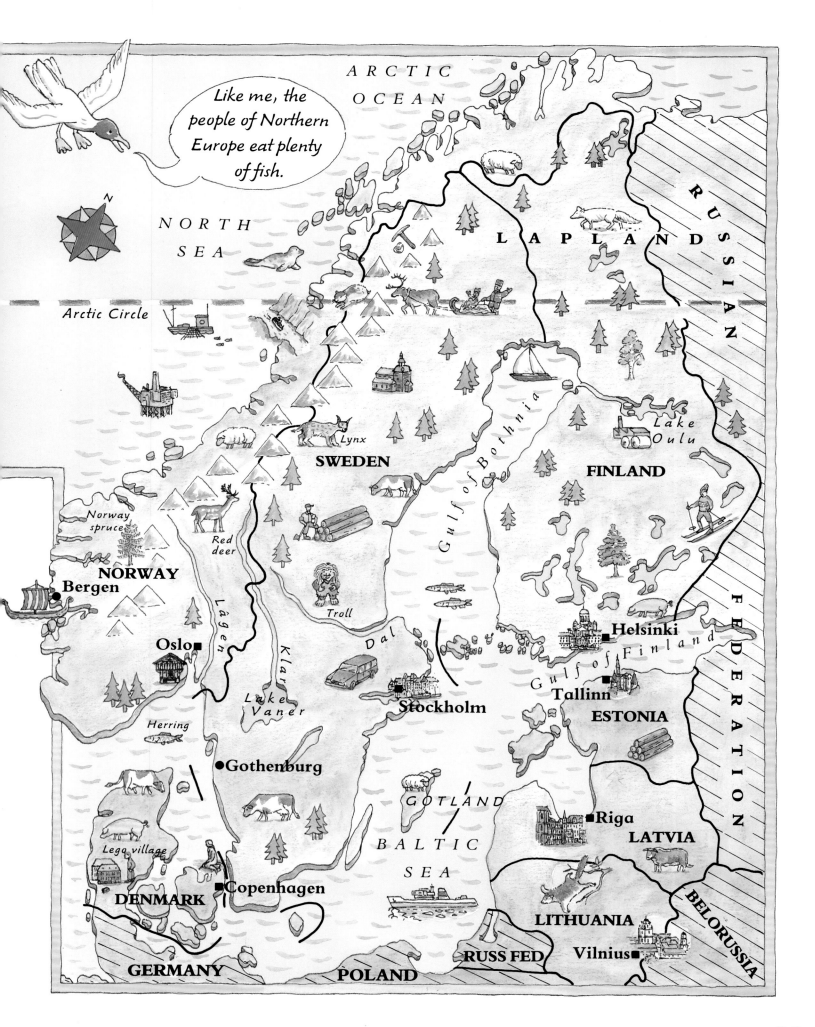

Like me, the people of Northern Europe eat plenty of fish.

ARCTIC OCEAN

NORTH SEA

Arctic Circle

N

RUSSIAN

LAPLAND

Lake Oulu

SWEDEN

FINLAND

Gulf of Bothnia

Norway spruce

Lynx

Red deer

NORWAY

Bergen

Troll

Oslo

Lägen

Klara

Dal

Helsinki

Gulf of Finland

Stockholm

Tallinn

ESTONIA

Lake Vänern

FEDERATION

Herring

Gothenburg

GOTLAND

Riga

LATVIA

Lego village

BALTIC SEA

Copenhagen

DENMARK

LITHUANIA

BELORUSSIA

RUSS FED

Vilnius

GERMANY

POLAND

29

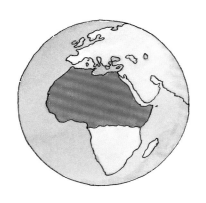

NORTHERN AFRICA

The vast Sahara Desert stretches across Northern Africa. Most people live south of the desert and around the coast. The land from Senegal to Cameroon used to be jungle but most of the trees have been cut down and crops such as coffee, cocoa and peanuts are grown instead. Many North Africans are Muslim, but others follow African religions and customs.

Can you see?

an oasis

the Great mosque at Mali

a house made of mud and straw

drums

a scorpion

cocoa pods

yams

a Tuareg child

an oil well

a jerboa

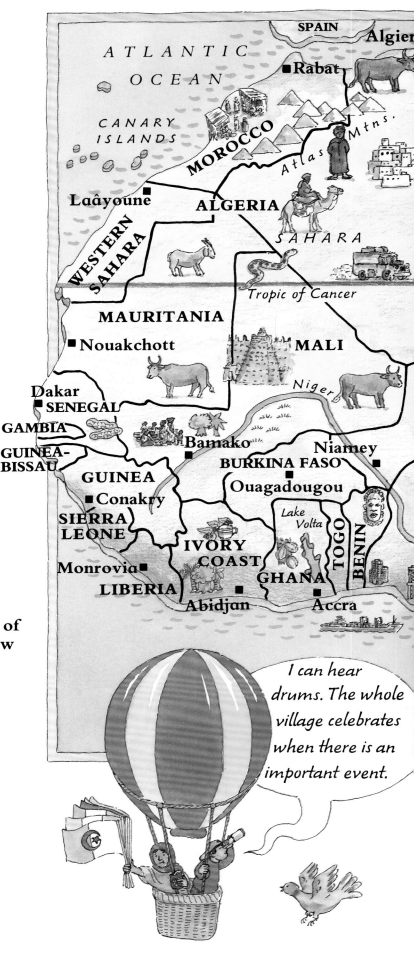

I can hear drums. The whole village celebrates when there is an important event.

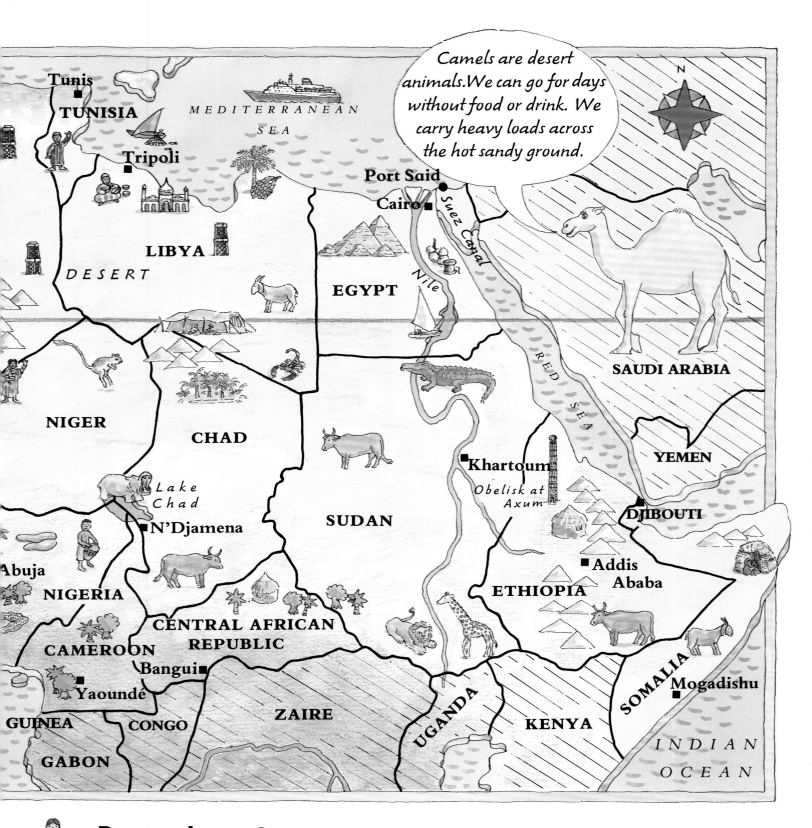

Camels are desert animals. We can go for days without food or drink. We carry heavy loads across the hot sandy ground.

N

Tunis
TUNISIA
Tripoli
MEDITERRANEAN SEA
LIBYA
DESERT
NIGER
CHAD
Lake Chad
N'Djamena
Abuja
NIGERIA
CAMEROON
Bangui
Yaoundé
GUINEA
CONGO
GABON
ZAIRE
CENTRAL AFRICAN REPUBLIC
Port Said
Cairo
EGYPT
Nile
Suez Canal
SUDAN
Khartoum
Obelisk at Axum
ETHIOPIA
Addis Ababa
RED SEA
SAUDI ARABIA
YEMEN
DJIBOUTI
SOMALIA
Mogadishu
KENYA
UGANDA
INDIAN OCEAN

Do you know?

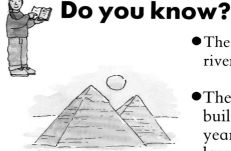

- The Nile is the longest river in the world.

- The pyramids were built around 4,000 years ago and are the largest stone buildings in the world.

- The Sahara desert is the world's largest desert and is getting bigger every year.

- The desert is scorching hot during the day and cold at night.

31

SOUTHERN AFRICA

Much of Southern Africa is high and flat. Farmers herd cattle on the grassy land in the East. Ferries and fishing boats sail on the big lakes. Giraffes and other wild animals live in the national parks. In the west, the Zaire flows through thick rainforest. Few people live in the deserts of Namibia and the Kalahari, but many work in the gold, diamond and copper mines.

Can you see?

Victoria Falls

Great Zimbabwe

Mount Kilimanjaro

Kariba Dam

a Masai farmer

a lemur

a black rhino

diamonds

an athlete

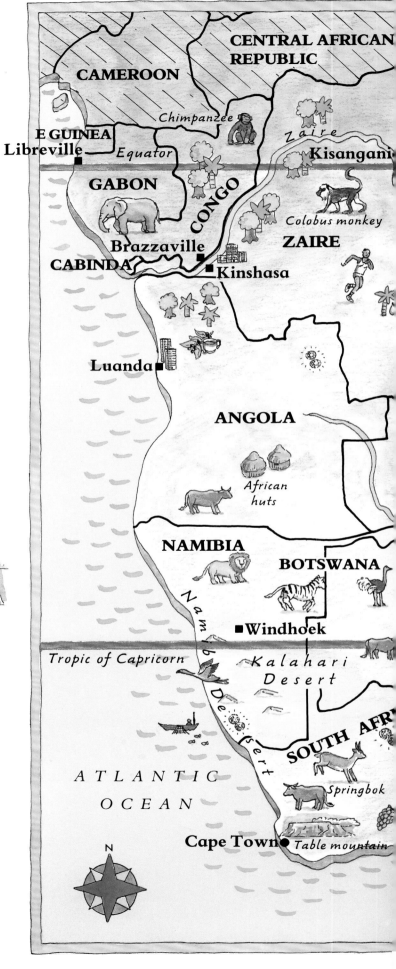

CAMEROON

CENTRAL AFRICAN REPUBLIC

Chimpanzee

E GUINEA
Libreville

Equator

Zaire

Kisangani

GABON

CONGO

Colobus monkey

Brazzaville

ZAIRE

CABINDA

Kinshasa

Luanda

ANGOLA

African huts

NAMIBIA

BOTSWANA

■Windhoek

Tropic of Capricorn

Kalahari Desert

Namib Desert

SOUTH AFR

ATLANTIC OCEAN

Springbok

N

Cape Town ● *Table mountain*

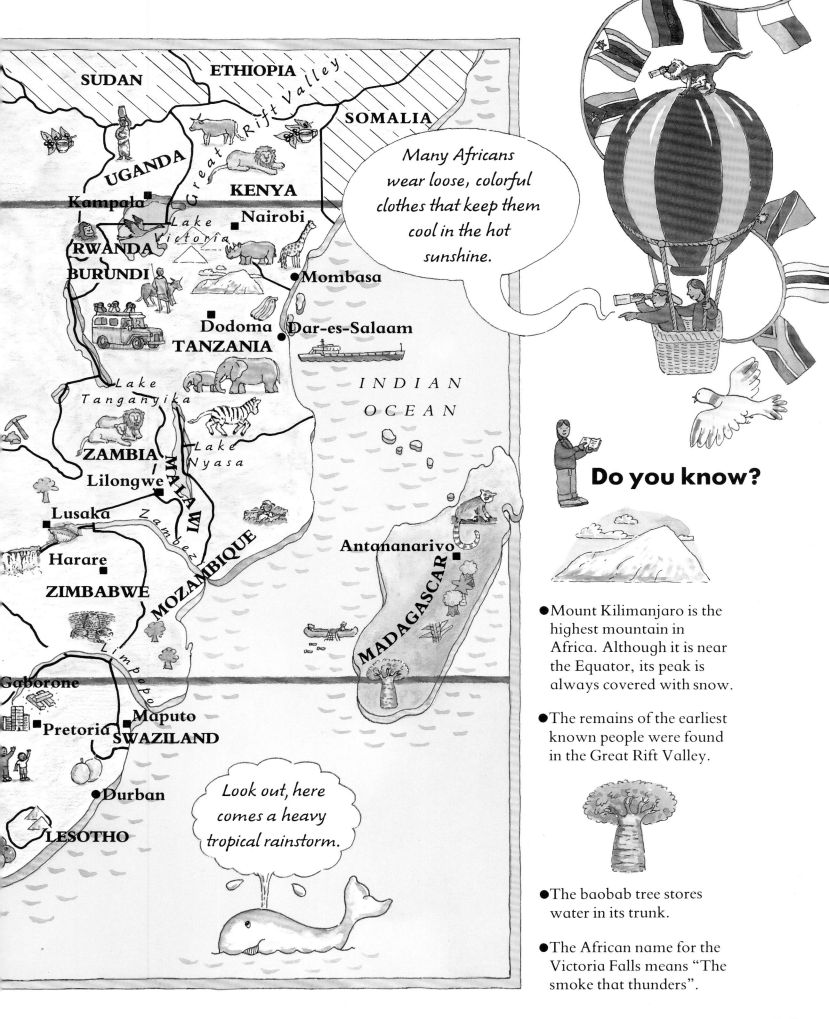

SUDAN

ETHIOPIA

Great Rift Valley

SOMALIA

UGANDA

KENYA

Kampala

Lake Victoria

Nairobi

RWANDA

BURUNDI

Mombasa

Dodoma · Dar-es-Salaam

TANZANIA

Lake Tanganyika

I N D I A N   O C E A N

Lake Nyasa

ZAMBIA

MALAWI

Lilongwe

Lusaka

Zambezi

Antananarivo

Harare

MADAGASCAR

ZIMBABWE

MOZAMBIQUE

Limpopo

Gaborone

Pretoria · Maputo

SWAZILAND

Durban

LESOTHO

Many Africans wear loose, colorful clothes that keep them cool in the hot sunshine.

Look out, here comes a heavy tropical rainstorm.

Do you know?

- Mount Kilimanjaro is the highest mountain in Africa. Although it is near the Equator, its peak is always covered with snow.

- The remains of the earliest known people were found in the Great Rift Valley.

- The baobab tree stores water in its trunk.

- The African name for the Victoria Falls means "The smoke that thunders".

33

RUSSIA AND HER NEIGHBORS

The Russian Federation is the largest of a group of countries sometimes called the CIS. Each country has its own language and customs, but most people also speak Russian. The Ural Mountains divide the Russian Federation. In the east, wolves, deer and bears roam vast pine forests and snowy wastes. Further south are grassy prairies. Most of the cities and farms are west and south of the Urals.

Europe and Asia meet at the Ural Mountains.

Can you see?

The Kremlin

The Winter Palace

Gateway at Samarkand

chess players

an elk

a sturgeon

Baikonur Space Center

a troika

a Georgian dancer

a gold mine

Do you know?

● The Motherland statue is the largest in the world. Her outstretched hand is large enough to hold an elephant.

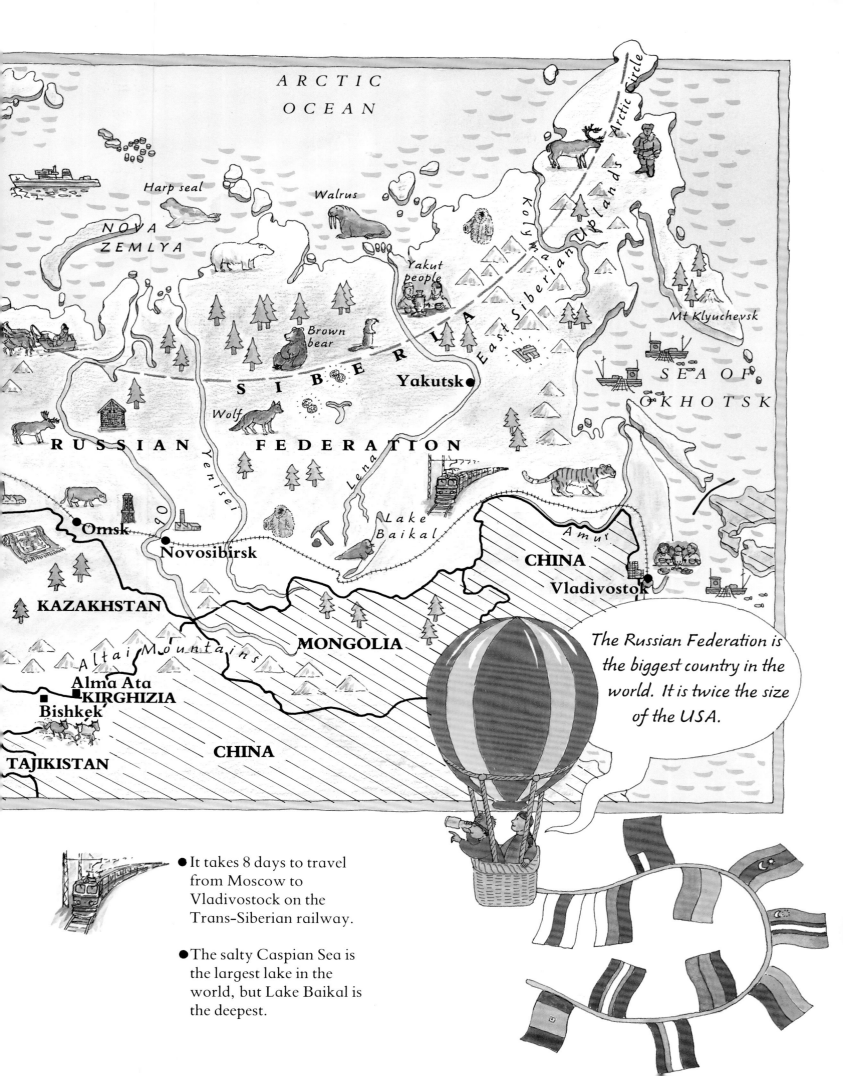

A R C T I C
O C E A N

Harp seal

Walrus

NOVA
ZEMLYA

Yakut
people

Kolyma

East Siberian Uplands

Mt Klyuchevsk

Brown
bear

S I B E R I A

Yakutsk

SEA OF
OKHOTSK

Wolf

R U S S I A N   F E D E R A T I O N

Yenisei

Lena

Lake
Baikal

Amur

Omsk

90

Novosibirsk

CHINA

Vladivostok

KAZAKHSTAN

MONGOLIA

Altai Mountains

Alma Ata
KIRGHIZIA
Bishkek

CHINA

TAJIKISTAN

The Russian Federation is
the biggest country in the
world. It is twice the size
of the USA.

● It takes 8 days to travel
from Moscow to
Vladivostock on the
Trans-Siberian railway.

● The salty Caspian Sea is
the largest lake in the
world, but Lake Baikal is
the deepest.

SOUTHWEST ASIA

Hot deserts stretch from the Sahara and the Red Sea across Southwest Asia. Crops grow only where there is water, around oases and near rivers. Oil wells pump oil up from deep below the ground. Huge tankers carry it all around the world. Northern Iran and the countries around the Mediterranean Sea are cooler and have more rain, especially in winter.

Can you see?

The Blue Mosque

a ziggurat

Turkish delight

a house made of reeds

a Bedouin tent

a camel driver

an oil tanker

a scorpion

an Arabian oryx

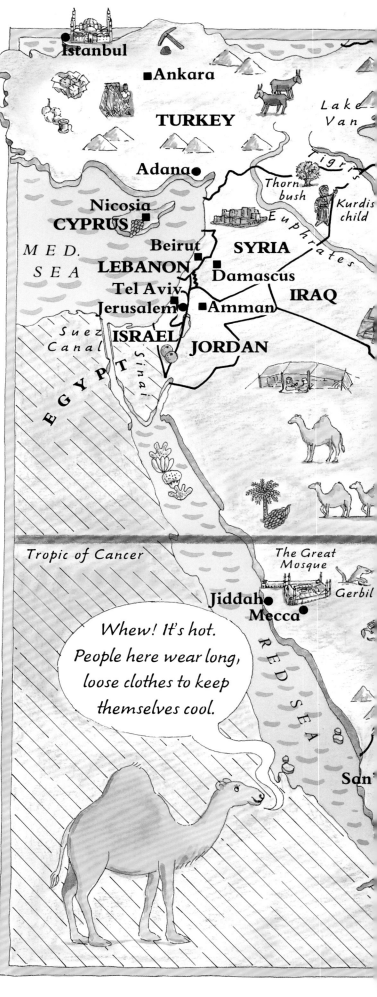

Istanbul

Ankara

TURKEY

Lake Van

Adana

Thorn bush

Tigris

Kurdish child

Nicosia

CYPRUS

Euphrates

M E D. SEA

Beirut

SYRIA

LEBANON

Damascus

Tel Aviv

Jerusalem

Amman

IRAQ

Suez Canal

ISRAEL

JORDAN

EGYPT

Sinai

Tropic of Cancer

The Great Mosque

Jiddah

Mecca

Gerbil

Whew! It's hot. People here wear long, loose clothes to keep themselves cool.

RED SEA

San

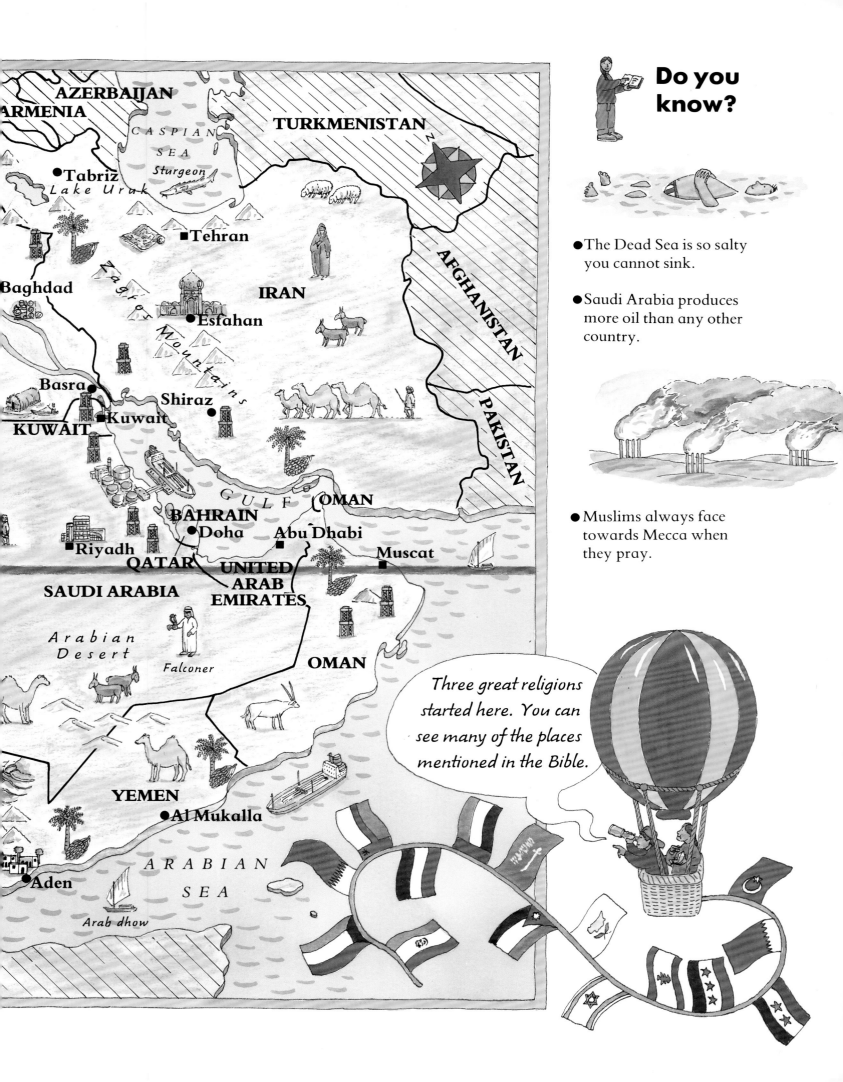

ARMENIA

AZERBAIJAN

TURKMENISTAN

CASPIAN SEA

Sturgeon

●Tabriz

Lake Uruk

■Tehran

Baghdad

Zagros

IRAN

●Esfahan

Mountains

Basra

Shiraz

Kuwait

KUWAIT

AFGHANISTAN

PAKISTAN

GULF

OMAN

BAHRAIN

●Doha

Abu Dhabi

Muscat

■Riyadh

QATAR

UNITED
ARAB
EMIRATES

SAUDI ARABIA

OMAN

Arabian
Desert

Falconer

YEMEN

●Al Mukalla

ARABIAN
SEA

●Aden

Arab dhow

Do you know?

- The Dead Sea is so salty you cannot sink.

- Saudi Arabia produces more oil than any other country.

- Muslims always face towards Mecca when they pray.

Three great religions started here. You can see many of the places mentioned in the Bible.

SOUTHERN and SOUTHEAST ASIA

These countries lie close to the equator, so the weather is either hot and dry, or hot and wet and steamy. Thick rainforest covers the mountains and islands of the southeast, but much of it has been cleared by farmers. Most people farm around small villages. They have few machines to help them with their work. The cities bustle with people, bikes, cars and animals.

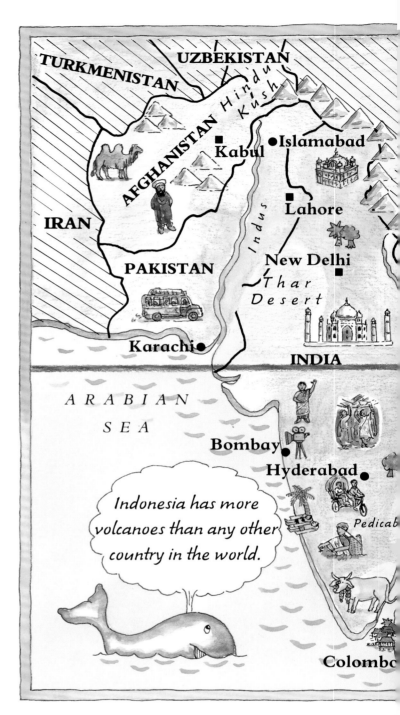

Indonesia has more volcanoes than any other country in the world.

Can you see?

The Taj Mahal

The Golden Temple

Mount Everest

a Bactrian camel

a Buddhist monk

a sacred cow

a Hindu festival

a bus

a Komodo dragon

a monkey-eating eagle

a flying fish

Do you know?

● Mount Everest is the world's highest mountain. There are 96 other peaks in the Himalayas which are almost as high.

● In the wet season, monsoon rains flood the land and the streets become like rivers.

● Hindus believe that the Ganges is a holy river. They travel there to bathe in the water.

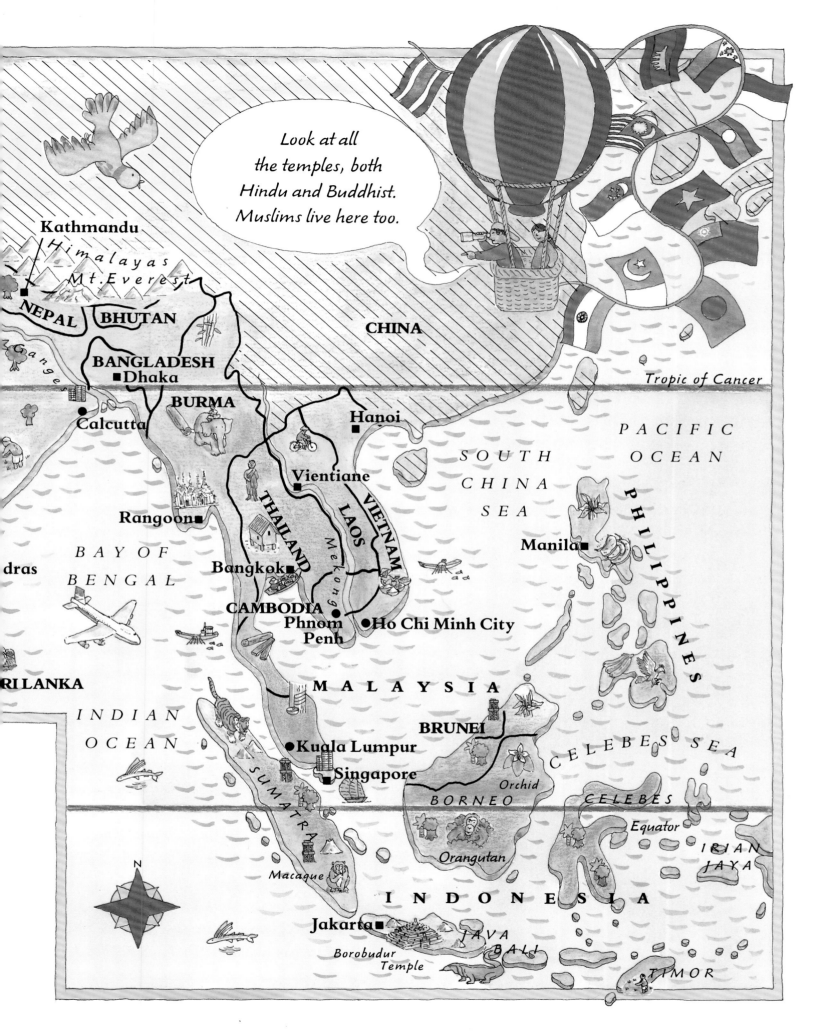

CHINA and JAPAN

China has more people than any other country, yet the land is mostly hot, empty desert or cold, high mountains. Most people live in villages on the flat plains in the east.

Japan is made up of several islands, with high mountains. Some of these are volcanoes. Most people live on narrow strips of land along the east coast. The cities are very crowded.

Can you see?

The Terracotta Army

The Great Buddha

The Temple of Heaven

The Potala Palace

Guilin Hills

a Japanese child

a Chinese dancer

a bicycle

a giant panda

a tiger

Japanese people do not shake hands — they bow instead.

KAZAKHSTAN

KIRGHIZIA

Takla Makan Desert

Himalayas

Tibetan Plateau

TIBET

Lhasa

NEPAL

INDIA

There are very few pandas left. The bamboo we eat is disappearing fast.

Tropic of Cancer

BURMA

Did you know?

- Chinese and Japanese people eat their food with chopsticks.

- One fifth of the world's population lives in China.

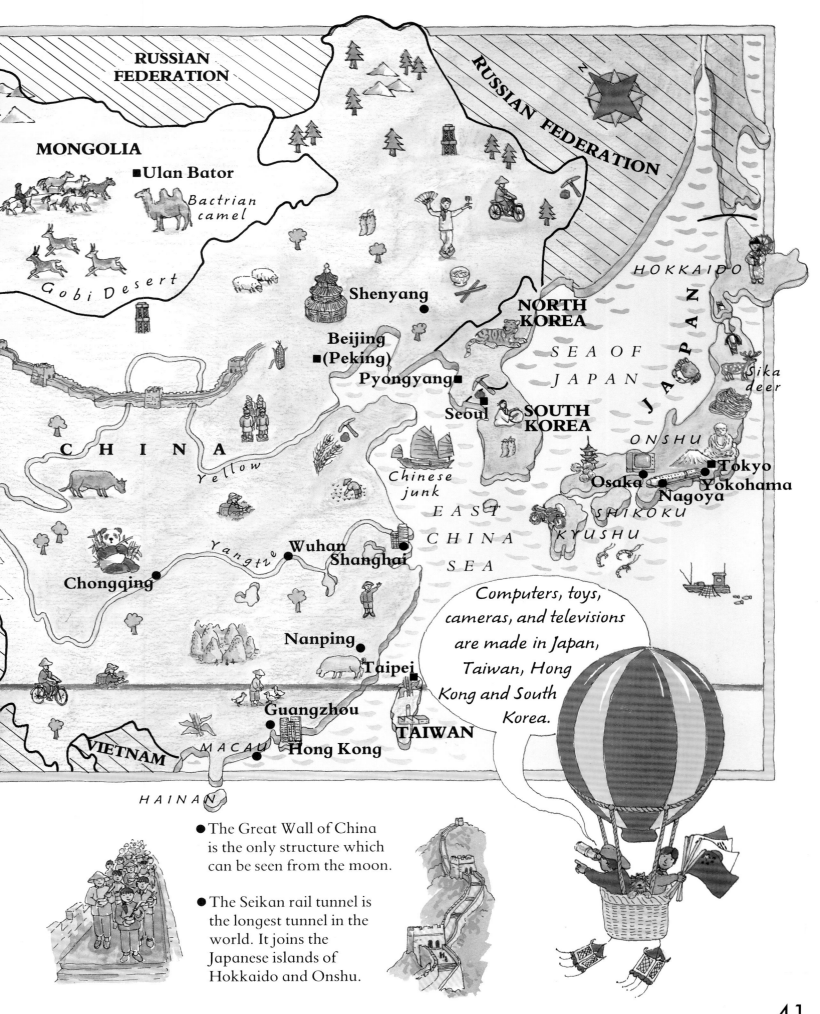

RUSSIAN
FEDERATION

RUSSIAN FEDERATION

MONGOLIA

■Ulan Bator

Bactrian camel

Gobi Desert

Shenyang

Beijing
(Peking)

Pyongyang ■

NORTH
KOREA

Seoul ■ SOUTH
KOREA

*SEA OF
JAPAN*

HOKKAIDO

J A P A N

Sika deer

ONSHU

CHINA

Yellow

*Chinese
junk*

*E A S T
C H I N A
S E A*

Osaka ■ Tokyo
Nagoya Yokohama

SHIKOKU

KYUSHU

Chongqing

Yangtze

Wuhan
Shanghai

Nanping

Taipei

VIETNAM *MACAU*

Guangzhou

Hong Kong

TAIWAN

HAINAN

Computers, toys,
cameras, and televisions
are made in Japan,
Taiwan, Hong
Kong and South
Korea.

● The Great Wall of China
is the only structure which
can be seen from the moon.

● The Seikan rail tunnel is
the longest tunnel in the
world. It joins the
Japanese islands of
Hokkaido and Onshu.

41

AUSTRALASIA

Australasia includes thousands of islands in the Pacific as well as Australia, New Zealand and Papua New Guinea. The north of Australia is tropical rainforest, but inland is flat desert. Most people live in cities around the coast.

Both Australia and New Zealand have big sheep and cattle farms. They also have wild animals that are found nowhere else in the world.

Do you know?

- Australia is the largest island in the world and the smallest continent.

- The Great Barrier Reef is the longest coral reef. It is made of the shells of billions of tiny animals.

Can you see?

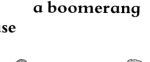

Ayers rock

Sydney Opera House

a boomerang

a surfer   **an Aboriginal child**   **a cricket player**   **a rugby player**

a flying doctor plane   **a Maori dancer**   **a tuatara**

- Ayers rock is a single huge outcrop of rock.

- The kiwi is the national symbol of New Zealand. It cannot fly and uses its long beak to stab the ground for worms.

INDIAN OCEAN

Darwin

Great Sandy Desert   *Lake Mackay*

A U S T R

Gibson Desert

W E S T E R N

A U S T R A L I A

Great Victoria Desert   *Dingo*

●**Perth**

Gum tree

GREAT AUSTRALIAN BIGHT

We have moved New Zealand closer to Australia to get it on the map.

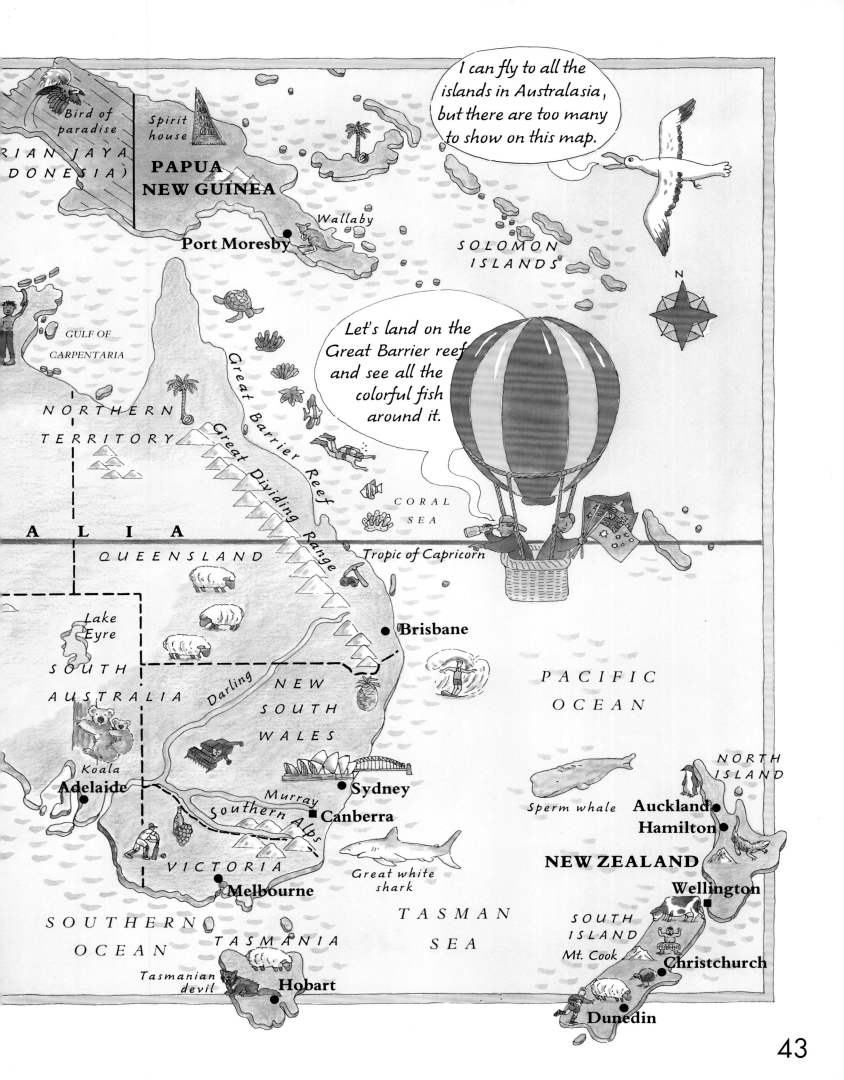

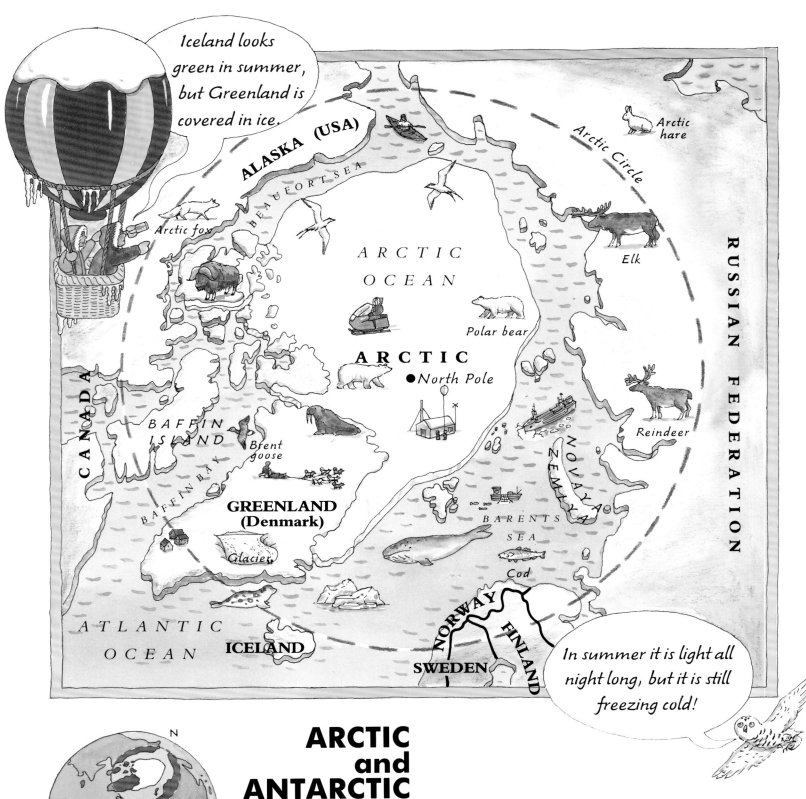

ARCTIC and ANTARCTIC

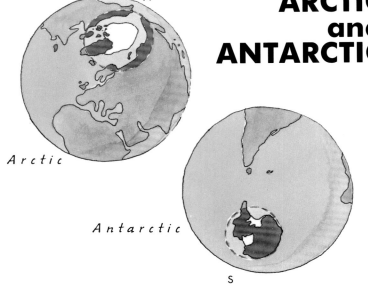

Arctic

Antarctic

The Arctic is an ocean of ice surrounded by land. Only summer is warm enough to melt some of the sea. The Antarctic is land surrounded by frozen sea. It is nearly twice as big as Australia but only seals and penguins live here all year round. No one owns this land and every country has agreed to preserve Antarctica as a wilderness.

Can you see?

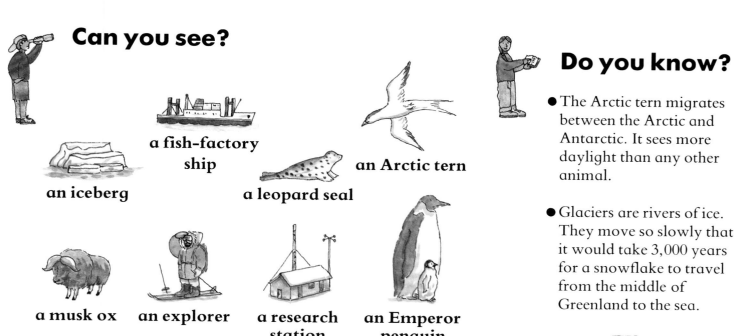

an iceberg

a fish-factory ship

a leopard seal

an Arctic tern

a musk ox

an explorer

a research station

an Emperor penguin

Do you know?

- The Arctic tern migrates between the Arctic and Antarctic. It sees more daylight than any other animal.

- Glaciers are rivers of ice. They move so slowly that it would take 3,000 years for a snowflake to travel from the middle of Greenland to the sea.

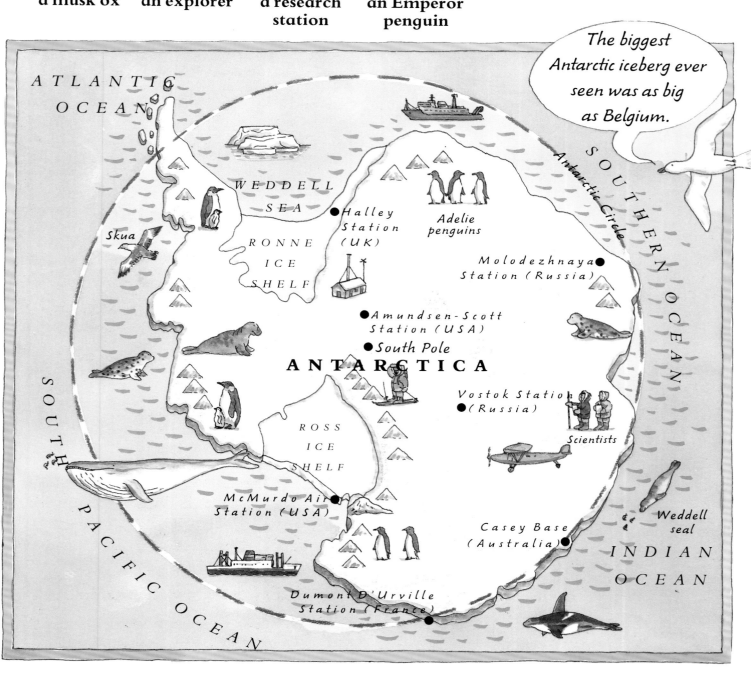

The biggest Antarctic iceberg ever seen was as big as Belgium.

ATLANTIC OCEAN

WEDDELL SEA

Skua

RONNE ICE SHELF

Halley Station (UK)

Adelie penguins

Molodezhnaya Station (Russia)

Amundsen-Scott Station (USA)

South Pole

ANTARCTICA

Vostok Station (Russia)

Scientists

ROSS ICE SHELF

McMurdo Air Station (USA)

Casey Base (Australia)

Weddell seal

SOUTH PACIFIC OCEAN

SOUTHERN OCEAN

Antarctic Circle

INDIAN OCEAN

Dumont D'Urville Station (France)

SOME FLAGS OF THE WORLD

 UK

 Rep. of Ireland

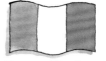 Denmark

 Finland

 Sweden

 Norway

 Iceland

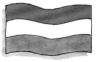 Netherlands

 Belgium

 Luxembourg

 Switzerland

 Austria

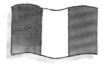 France

 Germany

 Italy

 Spain

 Portugal

 China

 Japan

 South Africa

 Malaysia

 Thailand

 India

 Pakistan

 Nepal

 Indonesia

 Zambia

 USA

 Canada

 Mexico

 Cuba

 Jamaica

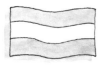 Argentina

 Brazil

 Peru

 Ecuador

 Colombia

 Chile

 Australia

 New Zealand

 Kenya

 Angola

 Guatemala

 Costa Rica

 Panama

 Poland

 Romania

 Hungary

 Algeria

 Zimbabwe

 Russian Federation

 Belorussia

 Azerbaijan

 Georgia

 Estonia

 Greece

Israel

Laos

 Jordan

Oman

Fun
FACTS

THE EARTH

Planet Earth is a ball of rock spinning through space. We live on the very thin surface crust of the planet. The inside of the Earth is very hot. There is a lot happening on the Earth's surface: mountains form, rocks are worn away, glaciers carve valleys, volcanoes erupt and earthquakes make it quiver and shake.

The **Earth** is not completely round. It is flattened at the Poles and bulges out in the middle.

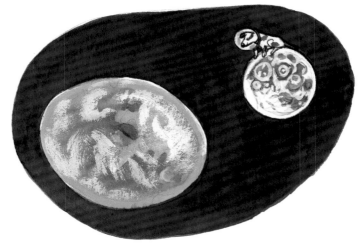

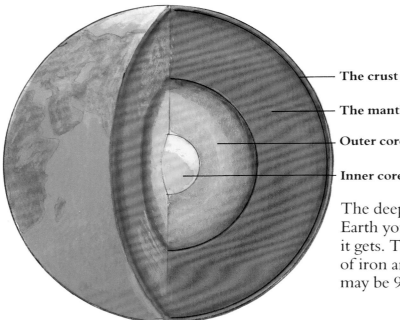

The crust

The mantle

Outer core

Inner core

The **icecap** in the Arctic Ocean does not cover land. It is a frozen sea, and submarines have gone underneath it.

The deeper into the Earth you go, the **hotter** it gets. The center is made of iron and nickel and may be 9000°F.

Glaciers are rivers of slow-moving ice. They can carve deep valleys. They can also pick up and carry huge rocks hundreds of miles.

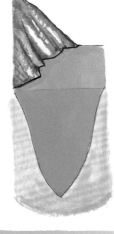

There are **deep trenches** in the oceans into which Mount Everest could easily fit.

HOW DID THE CONTINENTS FORM?
Millions of years ago the continents were joined together to form one big mass of land.

The continents of the world are moving very, very slowly. The Earth's hard crust is made up of separate sections, called plates. Beneath them the rocks are hot and liquid. The plates are moving on top of this molten rock.

Different kinds of rocks make up the Earth's surface and they are formed in different ways. Some, like **granite**, are made of molten rock which has cooled.

Granite

Sandstone

Marble

Marble is limestone that has been heated deep down in the Earth.

Sedimentary rocks, like sandstone, are made of layers of mud and sand, usually laid down in water, which then harden. They often contain fossils.

Chalk, a sedimentary rock, is made of the skeletons of prehistoric creatures.

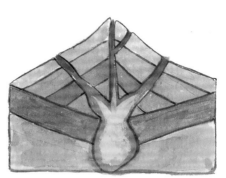

Volcanoes are openings in the Earth's crust. Hot liquid rock, called lava, pours out from below. **Erupting** volcanoes can hurl rocks as big as trucks into the air.

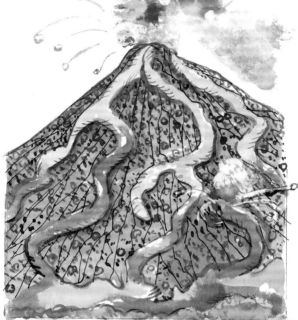

Rivers wear away rocks. **The Grand Canyon** has been formed by the Colorado River over 10 million years.

Geysers are spurts of water which has been heated in hot rock, deep below the Earth's surface.

Rocks can be worn into **amazing shapes** by sand blown in the wind.

As these plates move, they cause volcanoes and earthquakes. Earthquakes at sea can cause huge waves, called tsunamis, that are up to 76 yards high.

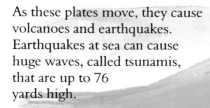

49

PREHISTORIC LIFE

Long, long ago, the earth was a very different place. Sea covered what is now dry land and was home to many of the creatures we now find as fossils. After a time, animals began to live on land as well as in the sea. Among them were the incredible dinosaurs. The first people appeared millions of years after the dinosaurs died out.

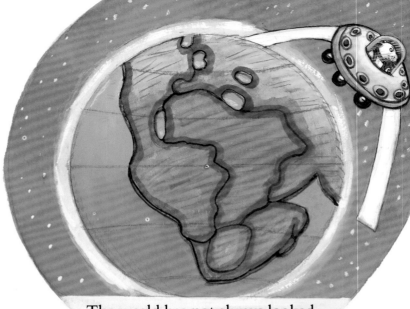

The world has not always looked the same. At one time, all the **continents** were joined together.

Fossils can be of teeth, bones, shells, plants, feathers, footprints, eggs, even droppings. From them we can learn about prehistoric life.

Huge dragonflies lived in the lush swamps of 350 million years ago.

Coelacanths are prehistoric fish. People once thought they were extinct, but one was discovered in 1938, and several found since, living off the coast of Southeast Africa.

Ammonites were prehistoric shellfish. Some were as small as a penny, others were as big as a car.

HOW ARE FOSSILS FORMED?
An animal or plant dies and falls to the bottom of the sea.

Layers of mud and sand cover it and gradually turn into rock. Parts of the animal are turned to stone.

The **dinosaurs** lived on Earth for about 160 million years. They died out suddenly 64 million years ago.

The largest dinosaurs were the plant eaters. **Brachiosaurus** was taller than a house.

Some plant-eating dinosaurs had **horns** and **armor**. These were for self-defence.

Fossils of droppings, called **coprolites**, can tell us what the animals ate.

Not all dinosaurs were huge. **Saltopus** was about the size of a chicken.

People who study **fossil footprints** can tell how fast the animal was moving when it made them.

Wooly mammoths lived a million years ago. Their bodies are still being found frozen in the ground.

In cold lands where trees cannot grow, early people made houses with **mammoth bones**.

Sometimes every part of the animal disappears. The hole that is left is like a mold. It fills up to make a cast exactly the same as the dead animal.

Amber is fossilized resin from ancient trees. Sometimes insects became trapped inside the resin and are preserved for us to see today.

THE WEATHER

There are lots of different kinds of weather. In some parts of the world the weather does not change much from day to day. In others, it can be hard to tell what is going to happen next. Whatever the weather, it is always made up of the same things: wind, water and heat from the Sun.

Cumulonimbus clouds can be as high as a mountain. They usually bring rain.

A **cloud** is formed of billions of tiny droplets of water or ice.

Lightning is a spark of electricity jumping between a cloud and the ground.

Weather vanes point into the wind. They show us where it is coming from.

Throughout history there have been people who believe that **dancing** can make it rain.

Some people believe that **windy weather** makes everyone bad-tempered.

HOW DO WE KNOW WHAT THE WEATHER WILL DO NEXT?

Weather forecasters get information from many different places. There are about 10,000 weather stations in the world. They record what weather they have.

From an airplane you can see that **rainbows** actually form a complete circle.

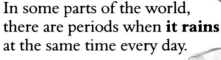

In some parts of the world, there are periods when **it rains** at the same time every day.

Hurricanes are called typhoons in Asia and willy-willies in Australia.

A **tornado** forms a funnel of wind which sucks up everything in its path.

Snowflakes always have six sides. No two are ever the same.

Hailstones the size of tennis balls once fell in Alabama.

Snowdrifts have been known to cover three-story buildings.

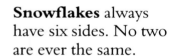

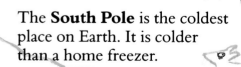

The **South Pole** is the coldest place on Earth. It is colder than a home freezer.

Balloons, satellites, radar and ships also take readings. Planes are used too. This weather plane is called 'Snoopy', because it has an extra large nose where the instruments are held.

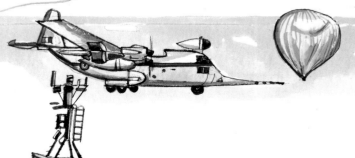

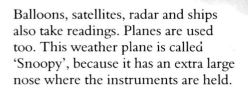

A WORLD OF ANIMALS

Planet Earth has just the right conditions for life. It is teeming with animals. They live mostly in the warm and wet places, but some animals can even live in the hottest and coldest areas. Scientists have so far found and named over a million different kinds. There are more yet to be discovered. Most of these will probably be insects.

Sloths have hair which grows backwards, because they spend their time hanging upside-down.

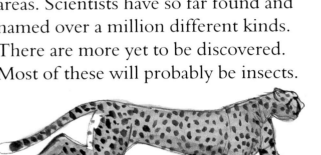

The **cheetah** is the only cat that cannot fully retract its claws. They give it grip for speed.

No two **tigers** have the same markings. Even the two sides of the same tiger are different.

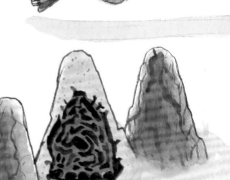

There are shafts and tunnels inside a **termites'** mound. Air runs through them to keep the mound cool.

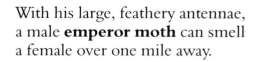

Marsupial animals give birth to tiny babies. They grow bigger inside a pouch on their mother's body.

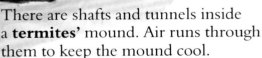

Some **cobras** spit venom at their enemies. They usually hit their target.

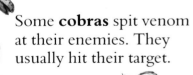

Mongooses can win fights with snakes, because they dodge and weave so much that the enemy does not know where to strike.

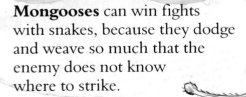

With his large, feathery antennae, a male **emperor moth** can smell a female over one mile away.

ARE HUMAN BEINGS THE ONLY ANIMALS THAT LIVE IN ORGANIZED GROUPS?

Some animals just move about or feed in groups. Others are more organized. Naked mole rats live in groups of about 30 animals.

Arrow-poison frogs have bright coloring to warn other animals that they are dangerous.

Bats use **echolocation** to hunt and find their way. They make sounds and, if these return as echoes, they know that there may be an object ahead.

Fossils show us that **tarsiers** have been on Earth for 45 million years.

Bees returning to a hive perform a dance which tells others where to find flowers with nectar.

Gorillas look dangerous, but they are peace-loving and strictly vegetarian.

Walruses use their tusks to pull their huge bodies out of the sea and on to land.

Nine-banded armadillos always give birth to four identical babies of the same sex.

The horn of a **rhinoceros** is not bone but keratin, the material of which hair and nails are made.

They build underground 'towns' of tunnels. There is one mole rat mother, who gives birth to all the babies. Others in the group dig the tunnels and bring food.

LIFE IN THE AIR AND SEA

The sea is home to millions of living creatures. Many of them are too small to see. Others are larger than any animals found on land. The skies too are teeming with life. There is an amazing variety of birds. They come in all shapes and sizes and have different ways of life.

Lapwings fly with dazzling acrobatics to attract mates.

The **black heron** makes an umbrella with its wings and catches fish beneath it.

Ospreys plunge into lakes and catch fish with their powerful gripping talons.

Salmon return from the sea to breed in the rivers in which they were born.

The largest animal on Earth, the **blue whale**, feeds on very small animals called krill.

Ocean sunfish lay as many as a million eggs.

DO FLYING FISH REALLY FLY?

There are fish that sometimes behave like birds. Flying fish try to escape from their enemies by leaping out of the water.

They use their tails to push themselves up out of the water.

They then glide along, using air currents, with their huge fins outstretched.

Emperor penguin chicks huddle together for warmth and safety. An adult looks after them.

Arctic terns fly across the world to the Antarctic when winter comes. That way they can enjoy two summers.

The magnificent male **frigate bird** has a large red pouch which he puffs out to impress females.

The **trunkfish's** body is protected by bony pieces in its skin that fit together like a box.

Each **humpback whale** has its own song and can hear another across hundreds of kilometres of sea.

Jellyfish catch their food with poisoned hooks on their tentacles.

The **male seahorse** broods his eggs in a pouch on the underside of his body.

The **sargassum fish** cannot be seen by its enemies because it looks like seaweed.

Some can cover distances of several hundred yards just above the surface, before entering the water again.

57

AMAZING PLANTS

We live on a green planet. Everywhere we go there are plants. They have been here longer than us and have developed some incredible ways of life. We use plants in every part of our lives and they provide us with the oxygen we need to live. There are hundreds of thousands of kinds of plants, living on land and in water.

All animals need plants. They make the **oxygen** that we breathe.

Evergreen trees lose their leaves gradually, so they never look bare, unlike deciduous trees which lose all their leaves in the fall.

A large **oak tree** can be home to hundreds of different kinds of insects.

Some trees produce seeds with built-in **propellers**. They spin away from the tree.

Some plants make new plants from parts of themselves, such as these **strawberry rhizomes.**

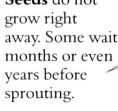

Seeds do not grow right away. Some wait months or even years before sprouting.

WHAT KINDS OF PLANTS DO WE USE?

These are some of the plants we use to make clothes, houses, fuel, furniture, paper, medicine, tools and, of course, our food and drink.

Cotton for clothes.

Timber for furniture.

The **mimosa** plant flops over if it is touched. In a few minutes it stands up again.

The **pitcher plant** catches insects for its food. The insects fall into the water-filled pitcher.

The leaves of the **Victoria water lily** are very strong. A child could sit on them.

Coconuts are seeds. They can float in the sea for many miles before taking root on a beach.

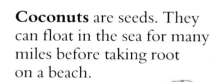

The **giant rafflesia** gets its food from other plants. It does not have leaves.

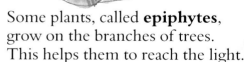

Some plants, called **epiphytes**, grow on the branches of trees. This helps them to reach the light.

Cacti can survive in hot, dry deserts. They store water in their stems.

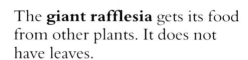

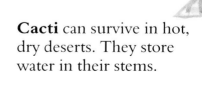

Tea, cocoa and coffee.

Aspirin from the white willow tree.

Soybeans for food and oil.

Bamboo plants for scaffolding.

BODY FACTS

Our bodies are amazing. We can run, jump, walk, sit, grip things and throw them. We can see, smell, hear and touch the world around us. We use our brains to store information and work out problems, and we can tell each other what we have found out. No one has yet invented a machine which is better than the human body.

There are 206 **bones** in the adult human body. The biggest are in the legs.

The **liver** is a very important organ. It does about 500 different jobs. One of them is to cause chemical changes to take place in broken-down food so that other organs can make use of it.

The **kidneys** clean the blood, taking out waste.

The **intestines** form a long tube, coiled inside the belly, in which much of our food is broken down. In adults the intestines are about 22 feet long.

Our **brains** can store over 100 million pieces of information. Nerves that spread all over the body carry messages to the brain.

The **lungs** contain about 300 million tiny air sacs, called alveoli, where the blood takes in oxygen and expels carbon dioxide.

The **heart** beats about 100,000 times a day, every day, for the whole of a human life.

The **stomach** is a bag of acid that breaks down food.

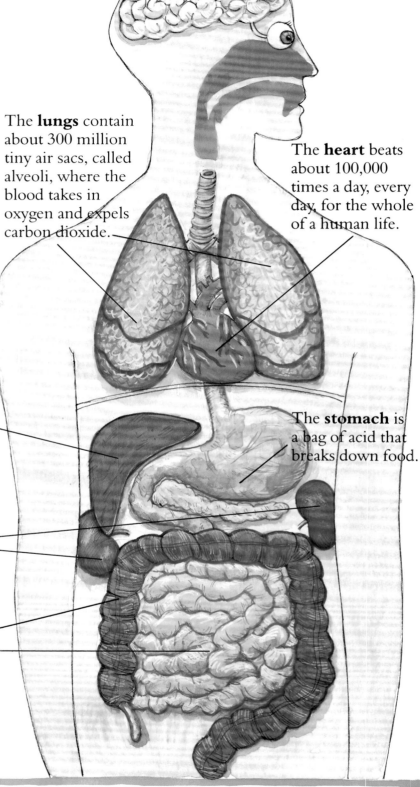

HOW DO WE GET ENERGY FROM FOOD?

The food we eat acts as fuel for our bodies. Some of it is used to replace body cells, and some to give us energy.

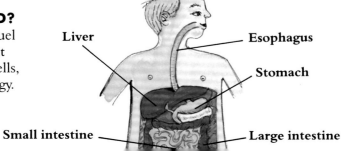

Liver

Esophagus

Stomach

Small intestine

Large intestine

Food starts to be broken down in our mouths, when we chew it with our teeth. It is then changed into sugars and other substances as it passes through our stomachs and intestines. This is done by powerful chemicals called enzymes.

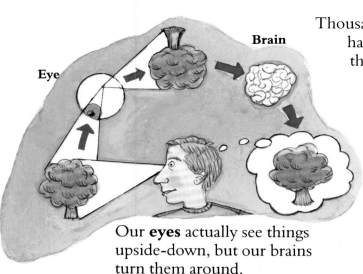

Eye **Brain**

Our **eyes** actually see things upside-down, but our brains turn them around.

Outer ear **Ear drum** **Inner ear** **Cochlea**

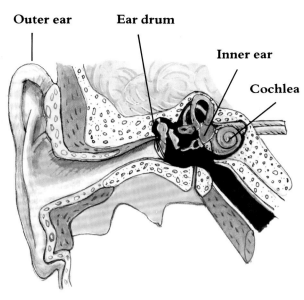

Thousands of microscopic hairs in the cochlea in the **inner ear** change sound waves into electrical signals, which are received by the brain.

Bitter **Sour**

Salt **Sweet**

Without our sense of **smell**, we would only taste four things, sour, salty, sweet and bitter.

A **sneeze** forces the air out of the nose at a speed of about 100 miles an hour.

We are made up of tiny **cells**. These die and are replaced as we grow older.

Hair **Muscle**

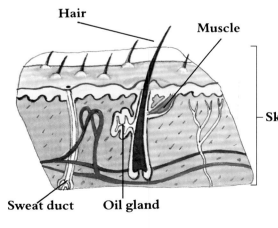

Skin

Sweat duct **Oil gland**

Goose pimples are caused by tiny muscles which swell and make our hairs stand on end.

Red blood cells **Bone cell**

Skin cell

Fat cell

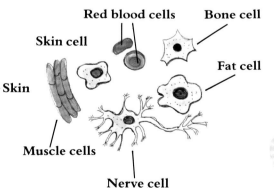

Muscle cells

Nerve cell

We **pant** when we run, because our muscles need extra oxygen.

There are hundreds of different **muscles** in the body. They move the body parts.

The sugars pass from the small intestine into the blood and are carried to cells all over the body. In the cells a chemical change takes place, and sugars are broken down using the oxygen we breathe in. This change releases energy. Our bodies use energy to do everything they need to do.

UNDER THE MICROSCOPE

Microscopes are used to make small things look bigger. As microscopes have gotten better and better, a whole world of detail has been opened up to us. They show us how everything is made of many small units joined together. They also reveal the extraordinary world of microscopic life which surrounds us.

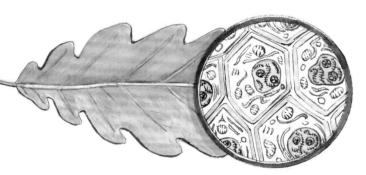

All living things are made up of tiny **cells**. This is a plant cell.

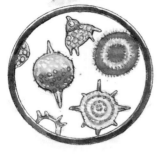

Radiolaria is a tiny animal made up of only one cell.

The **yeast** with which we make bread is a kind of fungus.

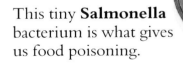

This tiny **Salmonella** bacterium is what gives us food poisoning.

Fungi produce **spores** which drift away in air or water. They then grow into new plants.

Plankton is made up of tiny plants and animals. It is food for many sea-dwelling animals.

WHO INVENTED THE MICROSCOPE?

The first microscope was made over 300 years ago by a Dutchman named Anton van Leeuwenhoek. He was the first person to see bacteria.

In light microscopes, light passes through an object and is bent by lenses. This makes the object look bigger.

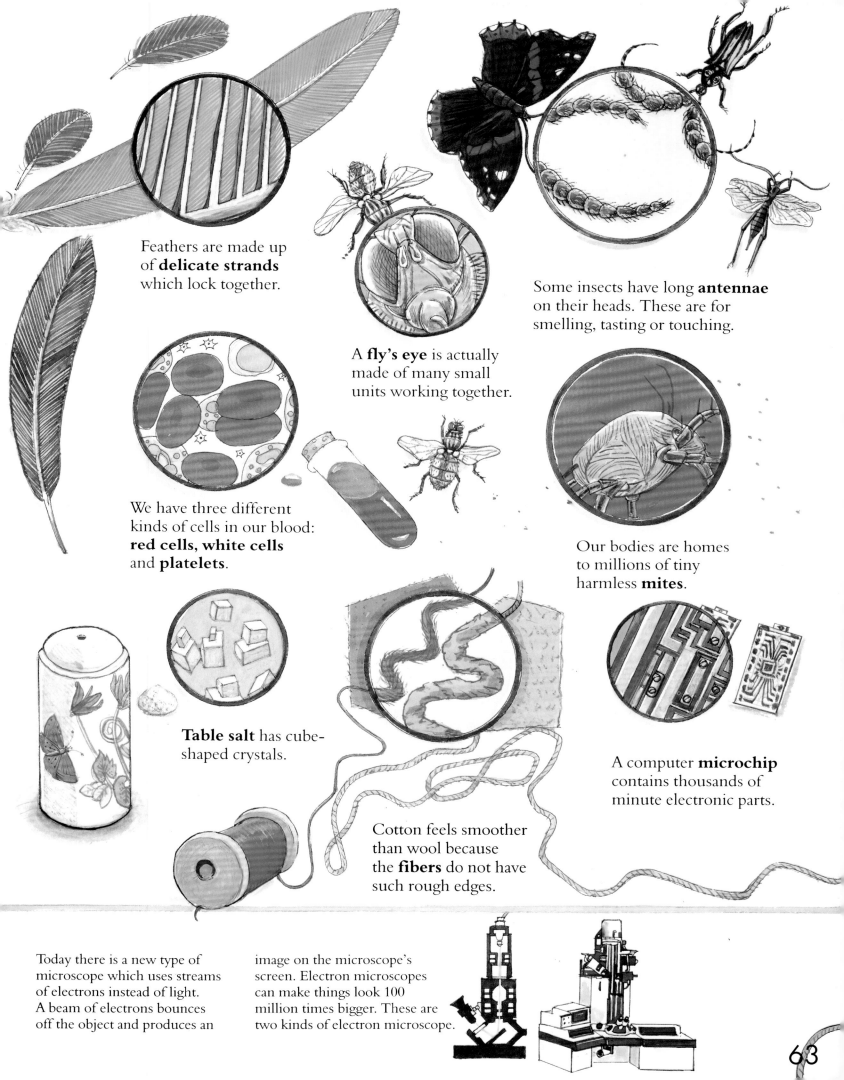

Feathers are made up of **delicate strands** which lock together.

A **fly's eye** is actually made of many small units working together.

Some insects have long **antennae** on their heads. These are for smelling, tasting or touching.

We have three different kinds of cells in our blood: **red cells, white cells** and **platelets**.

Our bodies are homes to millions of tiny harmless **mites**.

Table salt has cube-shaped crystals.

A computer **microchip** contains thousands of minute electronic parts.

Cotton feels smoother than wool because the **fibers** do not have such rough edges.

Today there is a new type of microscope which uses streams of electrons instead of light. A beam of electrons bounces off the object and produces an image on the microscope's screen. Electron microscopes can make things look 100 million times bigger. These are two kinds of electron microscope.

63

GETTING AROUND

Our distant ancestors traveled slowly on horses, coaches and carts, or just walked. For travel at sea they used boats with sails or oars. Today we get around with great speed in ships, cars, trains, trucks and airplanes of all shapes and sizes. Engines give power to most of these different kinds of transportation.

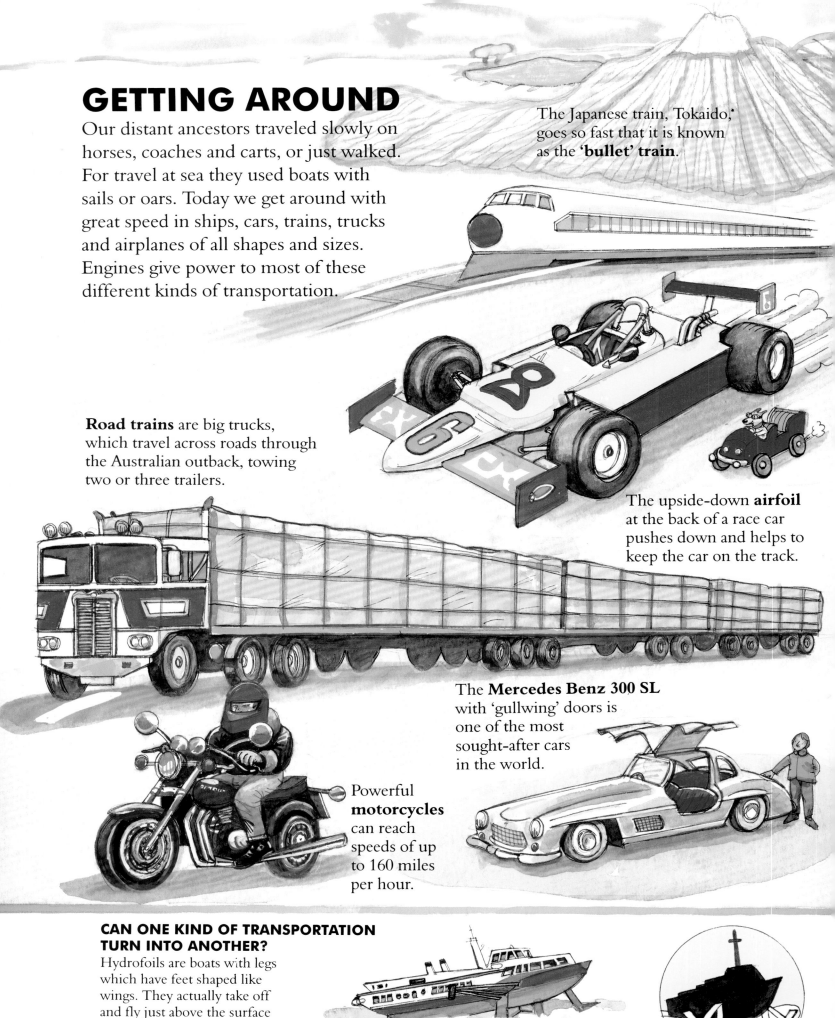

The Japanese train, Tokaido, goes so fast that it is known as the **'bullet' train**.

Road trains are big trucks, which travel across roads through the Australian outback, towing two or three trailers.

The upside-down **airfoil** at the back of a race car pushes down and helps to keep the car on the track.

The **Mercedes Benz 300 SL** with 'gullwing' doors is one of the most sought-after cars in the world.

Powerful **motorcycles** can reach speeds of up to 160 miles per hour.

CAN ONE KIND OF TRANSPORTATION TURN INTO ANOTHER?

Hydrofoils are boats with legs which have feet shaped like wings. They actually take off and fly just above the surface of the water.

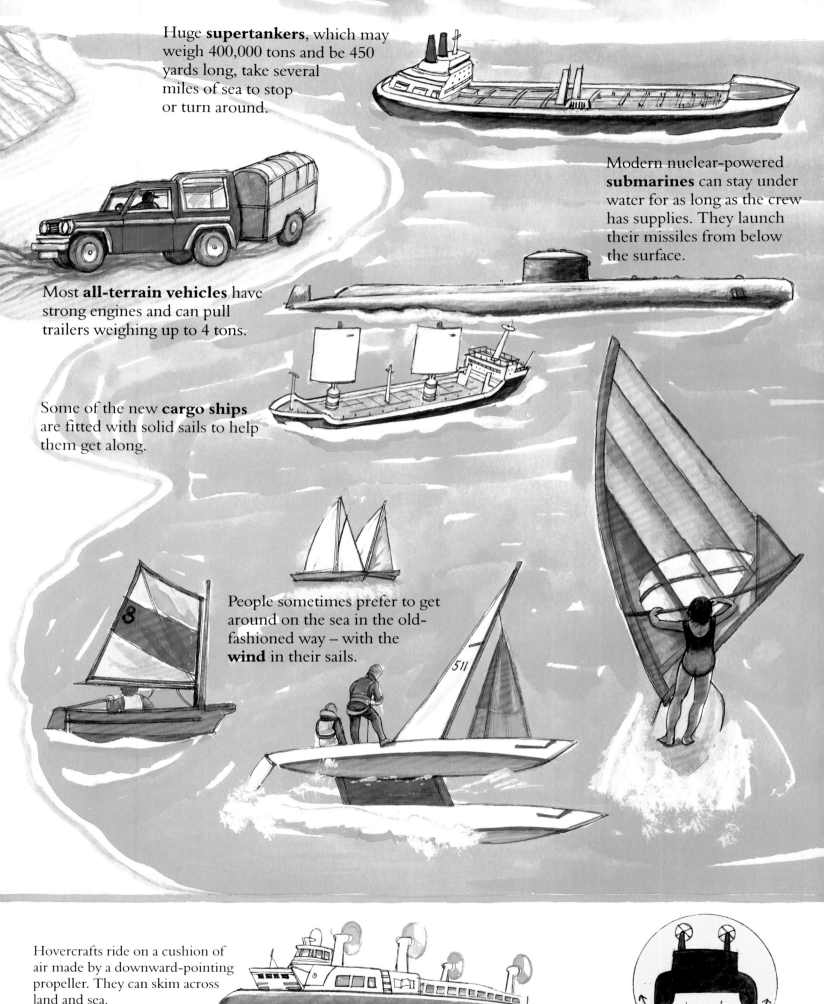

Huge **supertankers**, which may weigh 400,000 tons and be 450 yards long, take several miles of sea to stop or turn around.

Modern nuclear-powered **submarines** can stay under water for as long as the crew has supplies. They launch their missiles from below the surface.

Most **all-terrain vehicles** have strong engines and can pull trailers weighing up to 4 tons.

Some of the new **cargo ships** are fitted with solid sails to help them get along.

People sometimes prefer to get around on the sea in the old-fashioned way – with the **wind** in their sails.

Hovercrafts ride on a cushion of air made by a downward-pointing propeller. They can skim across land and sea.

Air

SPACE TRAVEL

For thousands of years, people looked into space in wonder. They may have dreamt of going to the moon. That dream came true in 1969 when Neil Armstrong became the first astronaut to walk on the moon. Since then we have taken photographs of other planets and now there are spacecraft going deep into space.

The **Sun** is at the center of our Solar System, which includes nine planets.

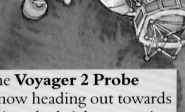

The **Voyager 2 Probe** is now heading out towards Sirius, the brightest star in the Solar System.

Mars is the closest planet to Earth. It has deep canyons and huge volcanoes.

Saturn's rings are made up of rocks spinning around the planet at high speed.

Comets develop long glowing tails as they get near the Sun.

Satellites orbit the Earth, doing a variety of tasks. This one looks at our weather.

WHAT IS LIFE LIKE IN SPACE?

In space there is no gravity. Things do not fall back to the ground the way they do on Earth.

Astronauts have to strap themselves to their seats when they want to sit down.

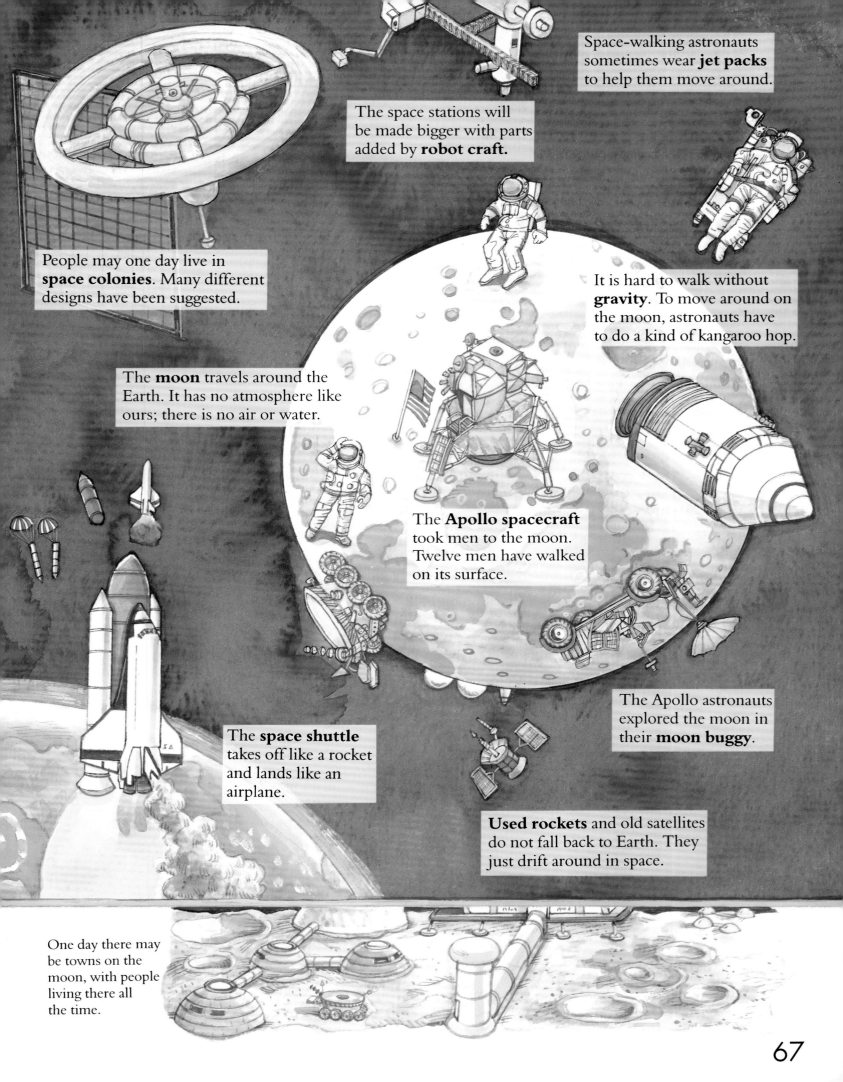

Space-walking astronauts sometimes wear **jet packs** to help them move around.

The space stations will be made bigger with parts added by **robot craft.**

People may one day live in **space colonies**. Many different designs have been suggested.

It is hard to walk without **gravity**. To move around on the moon, astronauts have to do a kind of kangaroo hop.

The **moon** travels around the Earth. It has no atmosphere like ours; there is no air or water.

The **Apollo spacecraft** took men to the moon. Twelve men have walked on its surface.

The **space shuttle** takes off like a rocket and lands like an airplane.

The Apollo astronauts explored the moon in their **moon buggy**.

Used rockets and old satellites do not fall back to Earth. They just drift around in space.

One day there may be towns on the moon, with people living there all the time.

UP IN THE AIR

People have always wanted to fly. At first, they tried with wings that flapped like birds. The wings were always too heavy. Now we know that fixed wings and, usually, an engine are needed. Today the skies are busy with many kinds of flying machine. There are airplanes, blimps, balloons, helicopters and gliders.

Rocket planes are the fastest planes ever. They have reached a speed of 4,546 miles per hour.

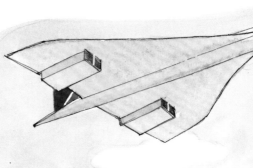

The **Concorde's** nose is lowered as it lands. This helps the pilot to see clearly.

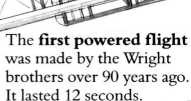

The **first powered flight** was made by the Wright brothers over 90 years ago. It lasted 12 seconds.

Gliders do not have engines. They are pulled into the air by other machines.

Helicopters can fly forwards, backwards, sideways, up and down. They can also hover in one place.

HOW DO AIRPLANES FLY?

The wings of an airplane are curved. The air passing over the wings moves faster than the air going underneath.

This creates air pressure pushing up from below.

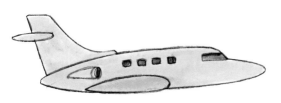

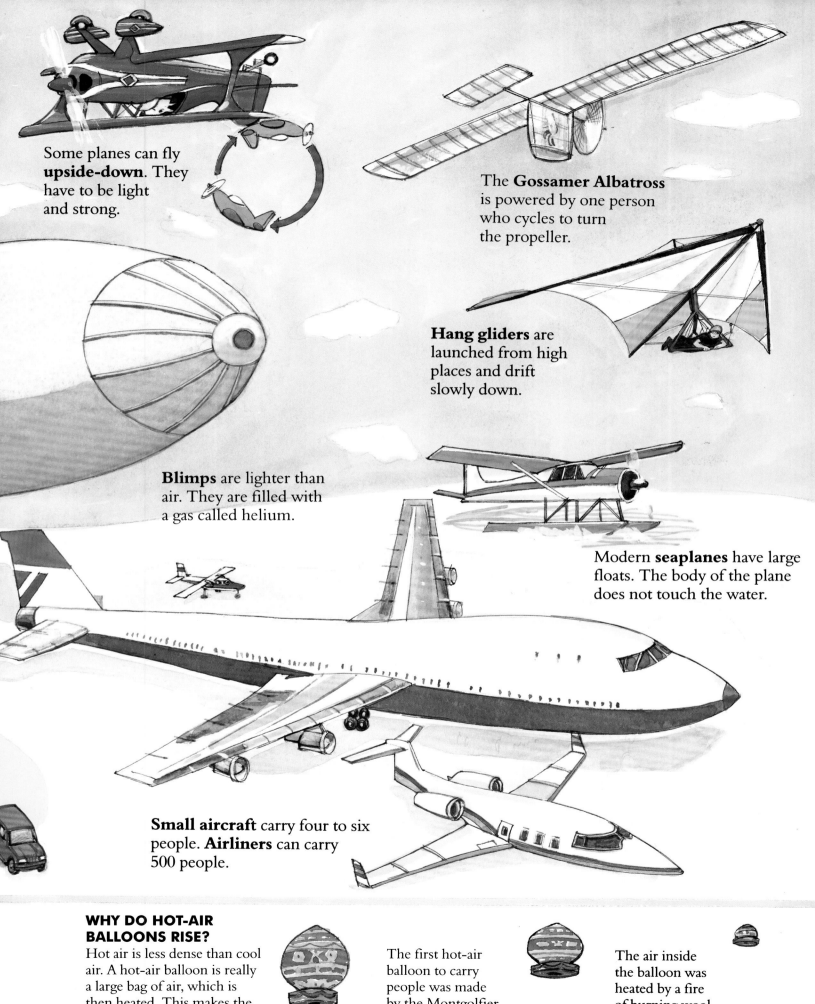

Some planes can fly **upside-down**. They have to be light and strong.

The **Gossamer Albatross** is powered by one person who cycles to turn the propeller.

Hang gliders are launched from high places and drift slowly down.

Blimps are lighter than air. They are filled with a gas called helium.

Modern **seaplanes** have large floats. The body of the plane does not touch the water.

Small aircraft carry four to six people. **Airliners** can carry 500 people.

WHY DO HOT-AIR BALLOONS RISE?

Hot air is less dense than cool air. A hot-air balloon is really a large bag of air, which is then heated. This makes the balloon lighter than the air around it, so it rises.

The first hot-air balloon to carry people was made by the Montgolfier brothers in 1783.

The air inside the balloon was heated by a fire of burning wool and straw.

PEOPLE OF THE PAST

Some people live lives that change the course of history. Military leaders have conquered lands; thinkers have changed the way we look at the world. Other famous people have changed the lives of ordinary people in small ways which made a big difference.

Alexander the Great (356-323 BC) was a king in ancient Greece. He won many battles and ruled a huge empire.

Suleiman (1494-1566) was Sultan of the great Ottoman Empire in the East.

The Polish astronomer **Nicolaus Copernicus** (1473-1543) worked out that the Earth went around the Sun.

Johann Gutenberg (1400-1468) was a German inventor whose machine with movable type made books easier to print.

Alexander Graham Bell (1847-1922) was a Scottish scientist who lived in America, where he invented the telephone.

Florence Nightingale (1820-1910) was an English nurse who tirelessly tended wounded soldiers. She started a school for training nurses.

The English scientist **Isaac Newton** (1642-1727) figured out that things always fall back to the ground due to the pull of gravity.

Louis Pasteur (1822-1895) proved how germs cause diseases, and then found ways of protecting people from germs.

WHAT ARE THE NOBEL PRIZES?

The Nobel prizes are awarded every year to people whose work is outstanding. They are named after Alfred Nobel, the man who invented dynamite. The prizes are for work in the sciences and arts. There is also one prize for work towards peace.

Some famous Nobel prize winners:

Pierre and Marie Curie for Physics (1903).

Elizabeth I (1533-1603) was one of England's greatest queens. During her reign there were many new discoveries.

Kublai Khan (1215-1294) was a great Emperor of China. He traded with Europe.

The Arab prophet **Mohammed** (570-632 AD) founded the religion known as Islam.

President Abraham Lincoln (1809-1865) fought against slavery in the American Civil War and made all slaves free in 1863.

Sitting Bull (died 1890) was a Sioux Indian chief who fought for his people's way of life.

Mahatma Gandhi (1869-1948) was an Indian leader who helped free India from British rule. He was against all kinds of violence.

Martin Luther King (1929-1968) was an American clergyman who worked for the civil rights of African Americans.

Guglielmo Marconi for Physics (1909).

Albert Einstein for Physics (1921).

Samuel Beckett for Literature (1969).

Mother Teresa for Peace (1979).

MOMENTS IN HISTORY

There are things happening in the world all the time. Most of them go unnoticed. Every now and then an event occurs which changes the course of history. It may be an event which marks the beginning of a new way of life for many people, or it may mean some other kind of change. Whatever type of event it is, people all over the world remember it.

People settled down and started **growing crops** for the first time about 12,000 years ago.

In 1783 the Americans won the **War of Independence** from Britain.

In 1620 people from England **landed in America** to start a new life.

In 1789 the French people **overthrew Louis XVI** and started governing their country without a king.

In 1845 one million people left Ireland due to famine caused by the failure of the **potato crop**.

In 1917 **Vladimir Lenin** became head of a new kind of government in Russia, where everything was to be run by the state.

In 1859 **Charles Darwin** shocked the world by saying that human beings had developed over millions of years from early ape-like people.

After millions had died, **World War 1** ended at 11 o'clock on the 11th day of the 11th month of the year 1918.

EVENTS AND IDEAS THAT CHANGED PEOPLE'S LIVES

Farming: around 10,000 BC - people began to tame and breed animals.

Getting around: 1820s - the age of steam travel began.

Joseph Lister

Preventing disease: 1865 - the first antiseptic spray was developed.

One of the world's earliest **cities** grew up in the fertile region called Mesopotamia in around 3,000 BC.

In around 598 BC, the **Buddha** became 'all-wise' and began teaching the beliefs known as Buddhism. In 6 BC **Jesus Christ** was born. He later gave the world the religion known as Christianity.

The great city of **Constantinople** fell to the Turks in 1453. Many scholars fled from the city and brought new learning to Europe.

In 1517 **Martin Luther** protested against the way the church was run and a new form of Christianity began.

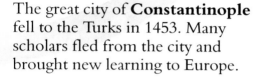

In 1989 the **Berlin Wall**, which had kept West and East Germany apart, was finally taken down.

In 1934-36 the Chinese leader Mao Tse-tung led the communists on the 593-mile **Long March** across China to escape from their enemies.

In 1994 **Nelson Mandela** became leader of the government in South Africa, and 46 years of apartheid came to an end.

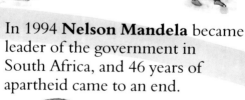

After years of protesting, all American women over 30 were given the **right to vote** in the elections in 1920.

In 1961, a Russian astronaut, Yuri Gagarin, became the **first human being** to see Planet Earth from space.

Waging war: 1945 - the first atom bombs were exploded in Japan.

Lifestyle: 1970s - the ecology-movement started.

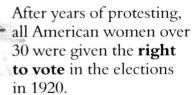

Getting in touch: 1980s - faxes, mobile phones and computers began to speed up communications.

73

AMAZING STRUCTURES

Long before the present day, people were building amazing structures. These were often religious temples or royal palaces, but people also built towers, bridges, tunnels, roads and dams. Thousands worked on them and they took a long time to build.

Huge stones were brought to **Stonehenge** in England from places long distances away.

The magnificent **Parthenon** in Greece was built over 2,300 years ago as a temple for a goddess.

The Mayans of Mexico, a long way from Egypt, built tall, **stepped pyramids** for their gods.

The ancient Romans were skilful engineers. They made massive **aqueducts**, which carried water over deep valleys.

The **Great Wall of China** is 2,514 miles long. It was built by slaves and many of them died during the 150 years it took to build.

The **Great Pyramid of Cheops** in Egypt is a tomb made of a million stone blocks.

In the Far East there are **huge stone statues** of the Buddha.

HOW WERE THE PYRAMIDS BUILT?
The Ancient Egyptians moved heavy stone blocks, using sleds, ropes and levers.

The blocks may have been pulled up ramps of earth, which were taken away once the blocks were in place.

People in the Middle Ages built many cathedrals with high roofs and splendid windows. This is **Notre Dame** in Paris.

The **Eiffel Tower** in France was once the world's tallest tower at 300 yards, but now the **CN Tower** (right) in Toronto, at 553 yards, is nearly twice as high.

The **Humber suspension bridge** in England has the world's longest span, of over 1,410 yards.

The **Statue of Liberty** in America is 93 yards high, from its base to the top of its torch, and it is hollow. You can climb up a spiral staircase inside.

The **Sydney Opera House** in Australia is made of huge concrete shells.

The Pei Pyramid in Paris is light and bright. It is made of 'high-tech' materials: steel and glass.

SCIENCE AND INVENTION

Science is the knowledge we gain by looking at and studying our world. We learn how it works and how the things in it are made. Inventors develop this knowledge to make things which are useful to people. Some inventions are made by just one person. Others come about slowly, over time, and are worked on by many people.

The **wheel** is probably the most important invention in history. It was first used over 5,000 years ago in Mesopotamia.

Galileo (1564-1642) was sent to prison for saying that the Earth moves around the Sun. He was right.

Jethro Tull's horse-drawn **seed drill**, invented in 1701, sowed crops in straight lines. This made them easier to weed and harvest.

Leonardo da Vinci (1452–1519) drew sketches for helicopters and tanks 400 years before they were actually made.

In 1877 Thomas Edison, one of the world's most famous inventors, recited 'Mary had a little lamb,' on the world's **first recording**. He also invented the **electric light bulb**.

SOME IMPORTANT INVENTIONS WHICH CHANGED PEOPLE'S LIVES

3000 BC - first sailing ships
3100 BC - bronze first used in Egypt
90 AD - first paper made in China

Compass

1125 - earliest known use of compass
1290 - first mechanical clock
1600 - first telescope
1712 - first steam engine

Telescope

The first gasoline-driven **four-wheeled car** was made in 1886 by Gottlieb Daimler.

In 1895, the scientist Wilhelm Konrad Roentgen took the first **X-ray**. It was of his wife's hand.

The first **TV camera** was made in 1925 by John Logie Baird, out of a tea chest, a cookie tin, bicycle lamps and darning needles.

Computer parts are getting smaller. Computers that once filled a room will now fit onto a table.

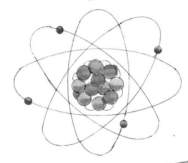

All objects are made up of tiny **atoms**. A speck of dust contains about 1,000 million, million atoms.

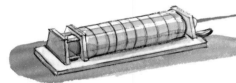

Laser beams can be used for eyesurgery, amazing light shows and for playing compact discs.

Sonar is a system using sound waves that humans cannot hear. These help to find shipwrecks and other objects underwater, by bouncing off them and sending back an echo.

Robots are used in factories and power stations to do a variety of difficult tasks.

Computers can create amazing images. With a **virtual reality** helmet and glove people can enter an exciting 3-D world.

1800 - first electric battery
1826 - first photograph
1903 - first aeroplane
1909 - first kind of plastic

Electric battery

1939 - first jet aircraft
1944 - first digital computer
1960 - first laser beams
1982 - first camcorder

Camcorder

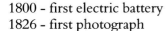
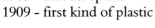

EXPLORERS AND DISCOVERERS

Explorers help us to learn about our world. They go to new places, open up new routes for trade, meet new people and study unknown plants and animals. In the past, some people traveled in search of wealth; others were looking for glory for themselves or for their countries. Others went in search of adventure and interesting discoveries.

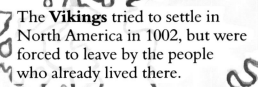

The **Vikings** tried to settle in North America in 1002, but were forced to leave by the people who already lived there.

In 1611, **Henry Hudson** and his son were cast adrift in a small boat by his crew. They were never seen again.

Five hundred years ago European sailors would not go past the Equator for fear of **monsters** and **boiling seas**.

In the 14th century **Ibn Battuta** crossed the dangerous Sahara desert. He went with traders, so that he would be safe from bandits.

Christopher Columbus was lost when he discovered the West Indies in 1492. He thought he had reached the East and was in India.

In 1835 the naturalist, **Charles Darwin**, saw birds and animals on the Galapagos Islands that did not exist anywhere else in the world.

The Portuguese captain, **Ferdinand Magellan**, set out from Spain in 1519 to sail around the world. Although he died, one of his ships completed the voyage.

WHY DID COLUMBUS SAIL WEST TO GET TO THE EAST?

Christopher Columbus was looking for a new way of reaching countries in the East, such as India and China. Many people of the time believed that the world was flat. Columbus thought it was round.

He believed that if he sailed west and kept going, he would eventually come to India. He was right, but he did not realize that North and South America were in the way. He accidentally discovered that they were there.

In 1871, a fisherman found a hut in the Arctic built by the Dutch explorer **William Barents** 274 years earlier. His ship had become trapped by ice, as he tried to travel east to China.

In 629 AD a Chinese monk named **Hsung-tsang** went traveling. He returned 16 years later in a chariot pulled by 20 horses and piled high with books.

Marco Polo left Italy for China in 1271 when he was 17. He was away from home for 24 years. On his return to Italy in 1295, he wrote a fascinating book about his travels.

Underwater explorers have visited the deepest part of the Pacific Ocean. It is about 7 miles down.

The explorer **Richard Burton** spoke 35 languages. In 1853, he traveled to Mecca disguised as an Afghan pilgrim.

Captain James Cook's famous voyage (1769-1771) was a scientific expedition to Tahiti, New Zealand and Australia. Over 700 species of plants were collected.

Mary Kingsley traveled alone in West Africa in the 19th century. She met African tribes and brought home many animals for others to study.

In 1911, **Roald Amundsen** and **Robert Scott** raced each other to the South Pole. Amundsen's Norwegian team won by five weeks.

Columbus made a further three voyages to the West Indies and South America. However the continents he found do not bear his name. They are named after Amerigo Vespucci, another Italian sailor.

SPORTS FACTS

Nearly everyone takes part in sport at some time in their lives. It keeps us fit, it is a challenge for our brains and it is great fun. Some sports are very old. They have changed over time and the rules have been fixed so that everyone knows how to play. Other sports are new and still developing.

In Korea people take part in **kite competitions** in which the aim is for one player to cross the line of another with his own.

When the first **Olympic games** were held in 776 BC, the sportsmen took part in events on their own, not in teams.

In 1389, the king of England banned **soccer**, because he wanted the people to practice their archery.

In the **Ironman triathlon**, the competitors have to swim 2.37 miles, cycle 112.5 miles and run 26 miles. It takes between eight and 12 hours.

The Aztecs of Mexico played a game like basketball, called **tlachtli**. Using only their knees and hips, they hit the ball through a stone ring.

HOW FAST CAN A HUMAN BEING RUN?

Since records began, people have been getting faster and faster. In May 1936, at the Berlin Olympics, the great American athlete, Jesse Owens, won three gold medals for running.

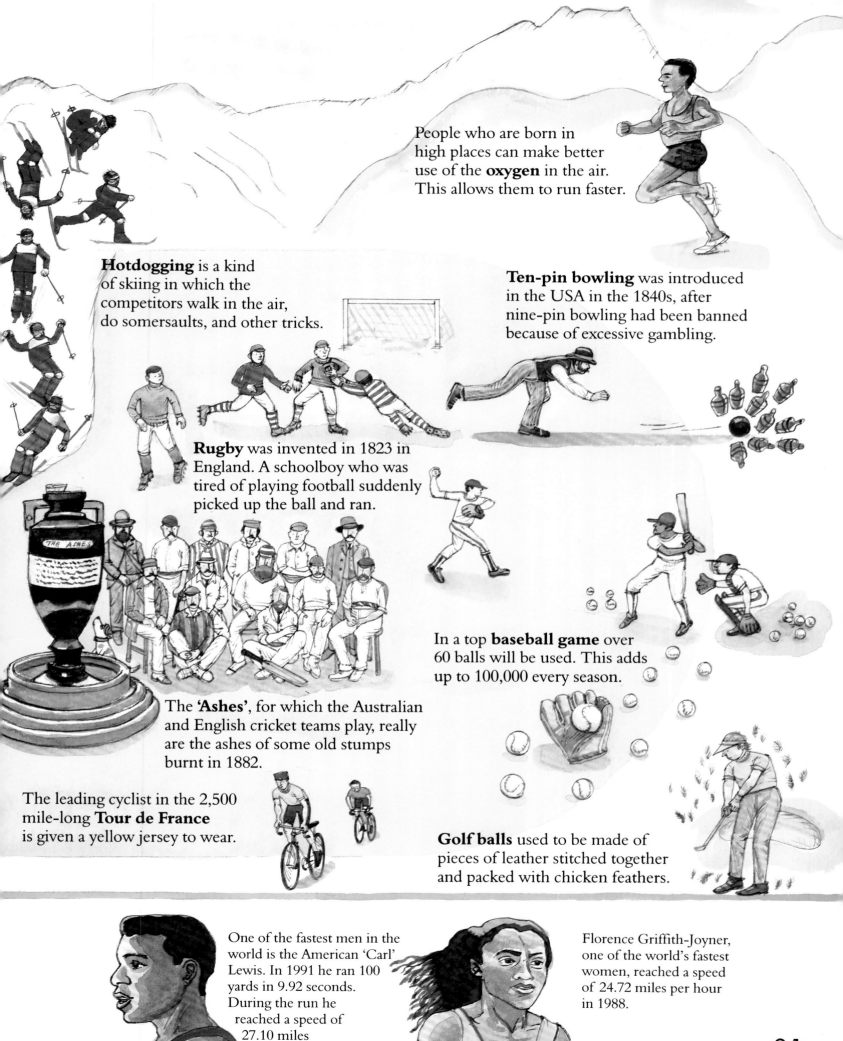

People who are born in high places can make better use of the **oxygen** in the air. This allows them to run faster.

Hotdogging is a kind of skiing in which the competitors walk in the air, do somersaults, and other tricks.

Ten-pin bowling was introduced in the USA in the 1840s, after nine-pin bowling had been banned because of excessive gambling.

Rugby was invented in 1823 in England. A schoolboy who was tired of playing football suddenly picked up the ball and ran.

In a top **baseball game** over 60 balls will be used. This adds up to 100,000 every season.

The **'Ashes'**, for which the Australian and English cricket teams play, really are the ashes of some old stumps burnt in 1882.

The leading cyclist in the 2,500 mile-long **Tour de France** is given a yellow jersey to wear.

Golf balls used to be made of pieces of leather stitched together and packed with chicken feathers.

One of the fastest men in the world is the American 'Carl' Lewis. In 1991 he ran 100 yards in 9.92 seconds. During the run he reached a speed of 27.10 miles per hour.

Florence Griffith-Joyner, one of the world's fastest women, reached a speed of 24.72 miles per hour in 1988.

81

HAVING FUN

There are many different kinds of art. Painting, writing, sculpting, playing music, dancing and acting are all kinds of art. We watch movies, plays and television shows, or listen to music, to be entertained. Sometimes we are also surprised or shocked. In this way we may learn something new about the world or ourselves.

Michelangelo Buonarroti (1475-1564) started painting the ceiling of the Sistine Chapel in Rome in 1508 and finished it four years later. He worked lying down, high up on a scaffolding.

Salvador Dali (1904-1989) made some unusual art objects such as a lobster telephone (seen here) and a sofa in the shape of a pair of lips.

The artist **Vincent Van Gogh** (1853-1890) really did cut off his ear after a quarrel with a friend.

The Greek sculptor **Phidias** made a huge wooden statue of the goddess Athene in the 5th century BC. It was covered in gold and ivory, and stood in the Parthenon in Athens.

In the 1960s, the Beatle **John Lennon** bought a Rolls-Royce and painted it with psychedelic patterns.

HOW DID THE OSCARS GET THEIR NAME?

The Oscars are awarded every year by the Academy of Motion Picture Arts and Sciences. They are given to actors, photographers, directors and others who make movies.

Humphrey Bogart

Vivien Leigh

Marlon Brando

Live Aid was a huge rock concert organized by Bob Geldof in 1985. It was one of the first to raise money for people in need.

Elvis Presley

The dinosaurs in the movie **'Jurassic Park'** were created on a very powerful computer.

When **Rock and Roll** first appeared in the 1950s, many older people were outraged by its loud and repetitive rhythms.

The composer **Ludwig van Beethoven** (1770-1827) wrote music even after he became deaf. He said that he could hear the music in his head.

The new **compact disc-interactives (CD-I)** will have music, film, information and games all on one disc.

In 1938, many people in America panicked when they heard a radio play, **'The War of the Worlds'**. The story was about Martians landing on Earth which was thought to be really happening.

One day, a librarian at the Academy said of the little golden statues, 'They look just like my Uncle Oscar.' The name has been used ever since.

On the night of the Academy Awards ceremony, crowds gather to see the movie stars arrive.

FACT QUIZ

Our friendly dog has had a busy time finding out all kinds of interesting things. However, there are a few facts he has forgotten to write down in his notebook. Can you help him?

1 How many young does the nine-banded armadillo have?

2 What is an ammonite?

3 What does the pitcher plant feed on?

4 Who took the world's first X-ray?

5 When did the French people overthrow their king?

6 Which is the closest planet to Earth?

7 How does the sargassum fish hide from its enemies?

8 What shape are salt crystals?

9 How did the Oscars get their name?

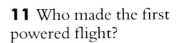

10 Who discovered that the Earth goes around the Sun?

11 Who made the first powered flight?

12 Who reached the South Pole first?

13 How many sides does a snowflake have?

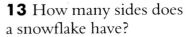

14 Which are the largest bones in the human body?

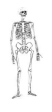

15 How many balls are used in a top baseball game?

16 What is a tsunami?

17 Which is the world's tallest tower?

Look for the answers within the pages of this book.

Amazing ANIMALS

ALL ABOUT ANIMALS

There are millions of different kinds of animals in the world. They live in all sorts of different places and they all do different things. Some are hunters, some eat plants, some can swim, and some can fly, and some can run very fast.

All the different kinds of animals belong to two main groups. One is the group of animals with backbones. The other is the group without backbones.

The animals with backbones are fish, birds, reptiles, mammals, and amphibians.

Mammals usually have fur and warm bodies and their young drink milk. You are a mammal. So is this bear.

Birds have warm bodies, feathers and wings (but they cannot always fly). They lay eggs.

Reptiles have dry scaly skins. Most reptiles lay eggs. Their bodies are only warm when they have been in a warm place.

WHERE DO all these different animals live?

Some live in our fields and farms,

some live in woods and forests,

others live in oceans, lakes and rivers.

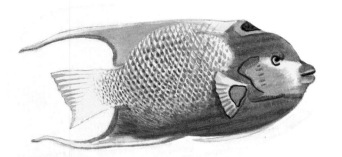

Fish live in water and breathe through gills. They usually have scaly skins. Most fish lay eggs.

Amphibians, like this frog, lay their eggs in water. The young live in water. Adults live in water and on land.

Many of the animals without backbones are very small. People sometimes call them 'minibeasts'. But some, such as octopuses and squid, can be large.

Insects always have six legs. Butterflies, beetles and flies are all insects.

Molluscs are a group of animals which usually have shells. Snails are molluscs. So are mussels and oysters.

Spiders have eight legs. There are many kinds of spiders. They are related to scorpions.

Animals with hard bodies, like lobsters and crabs, are called **crustaceans.**

This book will show you many different kinds of animals and how they suit the places they live in.

Some live in hot, dry places,

some like hot, wet places,

and others are found in very cold places.

ANIMALS IN OUR HOMES

People all over the world keep pets. We feed our pets and care for them. Some pets do useful jobs for us. Cats catch mice, and dogs can scare away burglars. But mostly, we keep pets just because we like them.

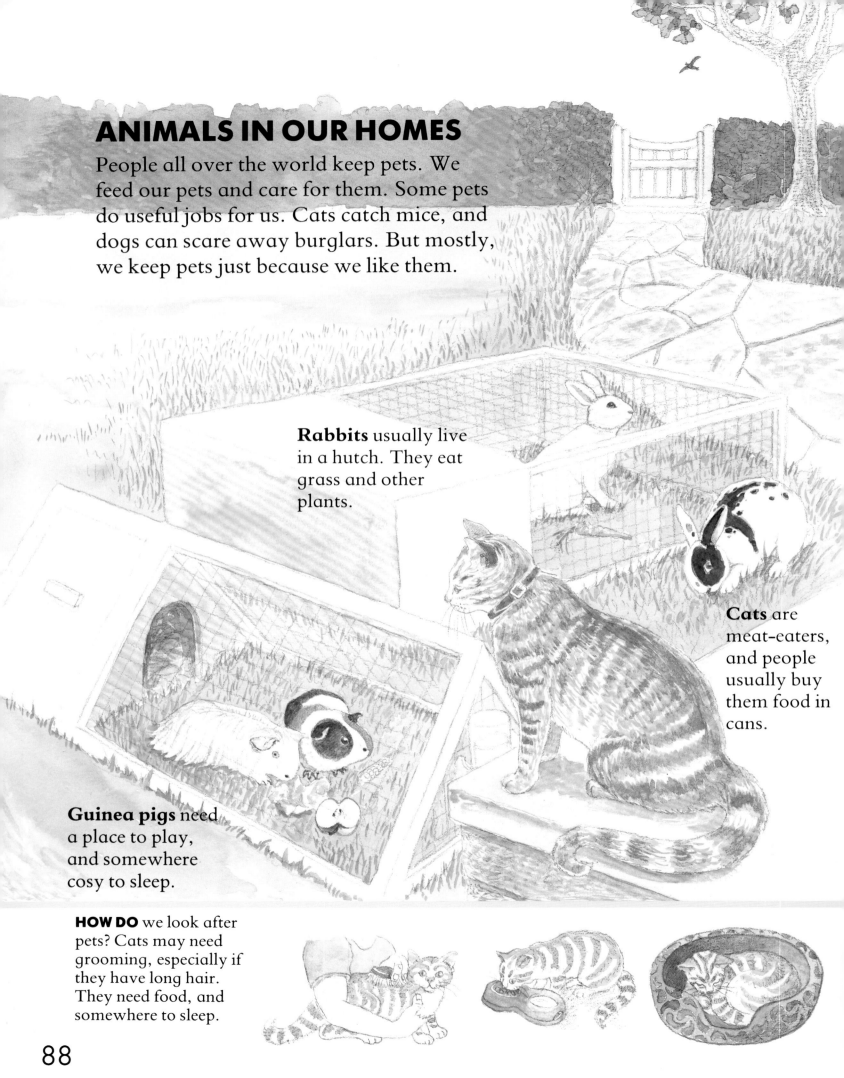

Rabbits usually live in a hutch. They eat grass and other plants.

Cats are meat-eaters, and people usually buy them food in cans.

Guinea pigs need a place to play, and somewhere cosy to sleep.

HOW DO we look after pets? Cats may need grooming, especially if they have long hair. They need food, and somewhere to sleep.

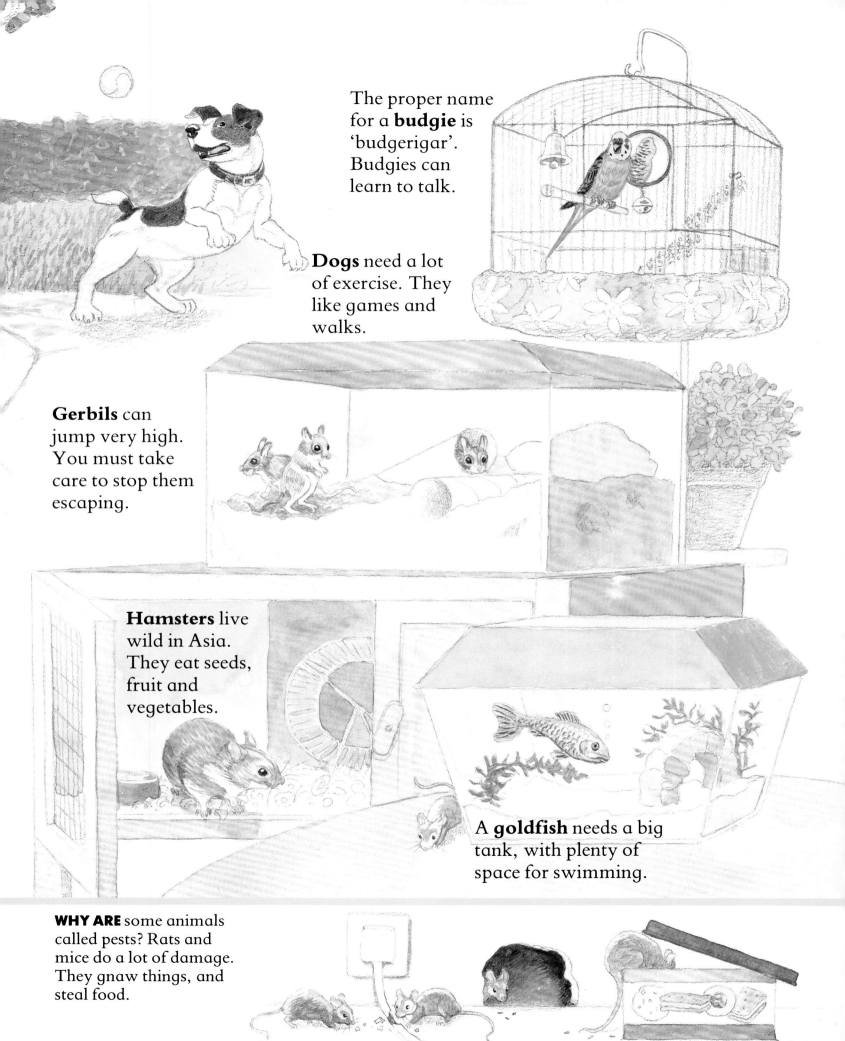

The proper name for a **budgie** is 'budgerigar'. Budgies can learn to talk.

Dogs need a lot of exercise. They like games and walks.

Gerbils can jump very high. You must take care to stop them escaping.

Hamsters live wild in Asia. They eat seeds, fruit and vegetables.

A **goldfish** needs a big tank, with plenty of space for swimming.

WHY ARE some animals called pests? Rats and mice do a lot of damage. They gnaw things, and steal food.

WORKING ANIMALS

Some kinds of animals work for people. Long ago, before there were cars, animals were used to carry heavy loads and to pull carts. Some animals still work in this way. Farmers keep animals because they give us meat, or other food such as eggs and milk.

In Asia, people milk **yaks** and use them to carry loads.

Farmers keep **sheep** for their wool. We use this to make cloth and sweaters.

Cows give us milk. A young cow is called a calf.

Donkeys are strong. They can pull carts and carry loads.

Chickens give us eggs to eat.

Ducks like to live near water. Young ducks are called ducklings.

HOW DO dogs help us? These sheep dogs are rounding up sheep. They can drive them to another field. The farmer shouts, or whistles, to tell the dogs what to do.

90

Camels are desert animals. They can go many days without food or water.

People from the mountains of South America use **llamas** to carry heavy loads.

Turkeys are big birds. They make a noise that sounds like "Gobble-gobble-gobble!"

Goats can eat very tough leaves and grass. Farmers keep goats for their milk.

Pigs like to dig in the soil with their snouts. Young pigs are called piglets.

People ride **horses**. Some large horses pull carts or ploughs. Young horses are called foals.

In snowy countries, people sometimes use teams of husky dogs to pull sleds. The dogs are strong and quick. The people shout to the dogs to tell them which way to go.

91

WOODLAND ANIMALS

Woods and forests are home to many kinds of animals. Some like woodlands, others live in the dark pine forests, and some can live in both. The animals in this picture live in the woods, forests and countryside of Northern Europe.

The **pine marten** hunts birds, steals eggs and eats berries.

Red squirrels live in pine forests and woodlands. They eat seeds and nuts.

The **tawny owl** hunts at night, for mice and other small animals.

Wild cats are bigger than pet cats and have thicker coats.

HOW DO toads breed? They lay eggs, called toadspawn, in water. Little black tadpoles hatch from the eggs. They look like fish, but they slowly turn into little toads.

spawn

young toads

tadpoles

92

Woodpeckers make holes in tree bark, and eat the insects they find there.

Wild boar search around beneath the trees, looking for roots and berries.

Fallow deer live in woodlands. The males' big horns are called antlers.

A **fox** can live almost anywhere – in woods, the countryside and even in town.

Badgers live underground. They come out at night to find food.

Toads hide all day and hunt at night, for slugs and snails.

Hedgehogs live in woods, fields and gardens. They eat insects.

HOW DO the hedgehog's prickles help keep it safe? When the hedgehog is afraid, it curls into a ball. Other animals leave it alone, because they do not want a mouthful of prickles.

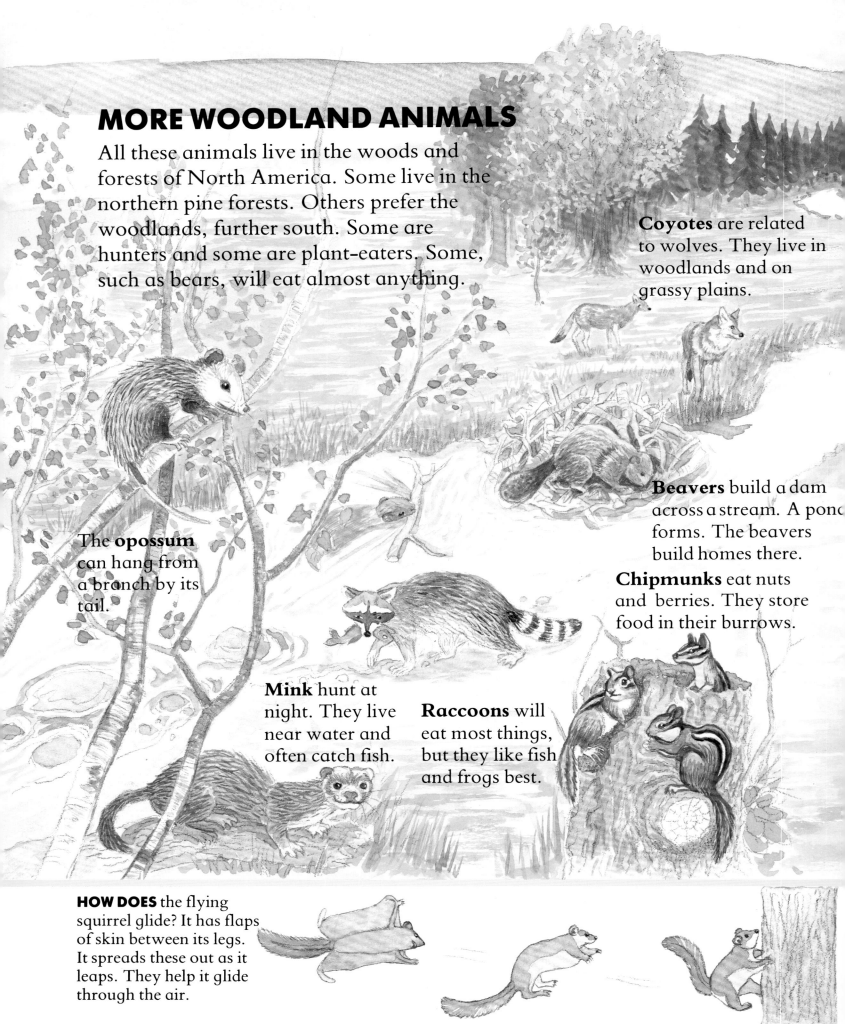

MORE WOODLAND ANIMALS

All these animals live in the woods and forests of North America. Some live in the northern pine forests. Others prefer the woodlands, further south. Some are hunters and some are plant-eaters. Some, such as bears, will eat almost anything.

Coyotes are related to wolves. They live in woodlands and on grassy plains.

The **opossum** can hang from a branch by its tail.

Beavers build a dam across a stream. A pond forms. The beavers build homes there.

Chipmunks eat nuts and berries. They store food in their burrows.

Mink hunt at night. They live near water and often catch fish.

Raccoons will eat most things, but they like fish and frogs best.

HOW DOES the flying squirrel glide? It has flaps of skin between its legs. It spreads these out as it leaps. They help it glide through the air.

Wolverines live in northern forests. They hunt other animals, such as deer.

This squirrel can glide so well that it is called a **flying squirrel**.

Black bears hunt deer sometimes. They also eat eggs, fruit and berries.

The **bobcat's** spotted coat makes it hard to see among the trees.

Porcupines have spines called quills. These protect them from other animals.

Blue jays live in northern forests, but fly south in winter.

Wild turkeys are related to the tame ones that live on farms.

HOW DO blue jays help plant new trees? They bury acorns, so they can eat them later. But they do not find them all and some start to grow.

GRASSLAND ANIMALS

These animals live on the savanna, the grassy plains of Africa. Some eat grass or leaves from trees. Others are hunters. Many grassland animals can run fast, to catch food or escape from danger. They often have coats the color of dry grass, to make them hard to see.

Giraffes are so tall they can nibble leaves at the tops of trees.

Lions live in groups called prides. They are fierce hunters.

Ostriches cannot fly, but they can run at 70 kilometres an hour.

Hippopotamuses spend all day in water. At night, they come out and eat grass.

Puff adders are poisonous snakes. They swell up when they are angry.

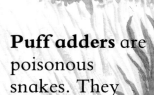

HOW DO lions hunt? The lionesses surround a herd of zebra and pounce on one of them. Then the lions, cubs and lionesses can all eat.

Vultures eat the remains of creatures killed by lions and other hunters.

When a **springbok** sees danger it jumps, to warn the rest of the herd.

African elephants eat bushes and grass. They live in groups called herds.

Jackals are a kind of wild dog. They live and hunt in family groups.

Oxpeckers eat the biting insects that live on the skin of buffalos.

Buffalo are big and keep cool by lying in the mud.

Vervet monkeys leap through the trees, making a lot of noise.

HOW DO animals feed in the same part of the savanna? The giraffe eats from the tree-top. The gerenuk nibbles leaves lower down. The gazelle eats the lowest leaves of all.

MOUNTAIN ANIMALS

Many different kinds of animals live in the mountains. Some live among the trees on the lower slopes. Others live higher up, on grassy and rocky slopes. The animals in this picture live in the mountains of Asia.

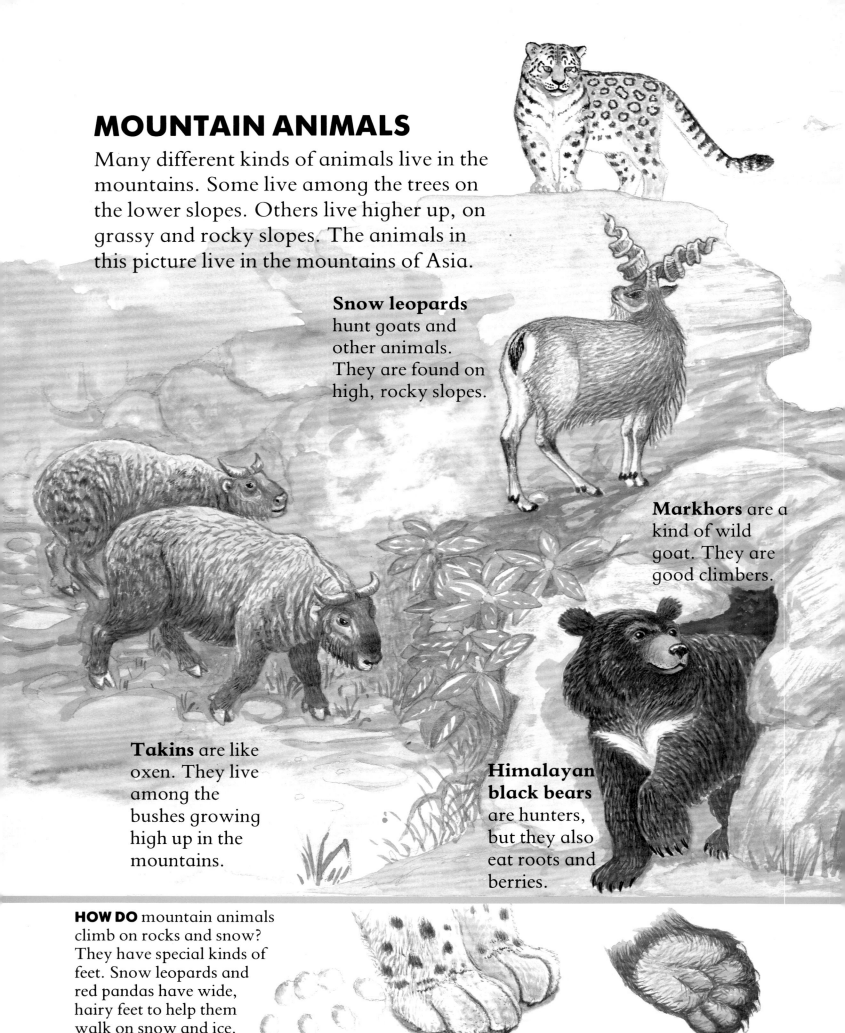

Snow leopards hunt goats and other animals. They are found on high, rocky slopes.

Markhors are a kind of wild goat. They are good climbers.

Takins are like oxen. They live among the bushes growing high up in the mountains.

Himalayan black bears are hunters, but they also eat roots and berries.

HOW DO mountain animals climb on rocks and snow? They have special kinds of feet. Snow leopards and red pandas have wide, hairy feet to help them walk on snow and ice.

98

Griffon vultures soar above the mountains, looking for dead animals to eat.

Argalis live in the high plateaus of Tibet. They are a kind of wild sheep.

Most **yaks** are kept by people, but there are a few wild ones left.

Langur monkeys live in mountain forests and leap from tree to tree.

Red pandas eat berries and small animals.

The **Bhutan glory** butterfly only shows its bright colors when an enemy gets close.

HOW DO the animals keep warm in winter? Marmots spend winter hibernating (sleeping deeply) in their burrows. Takins, and other animals, move to warmer, lower slopes. Yaks' coats are so thick that they do not mind cold weather.

DESERT ANIMALS

Deserts are difficult places for animals to live. There is not much water and few plants grow. The animals in this picture live in the Sahara desert, in Africa. Here, the days are burning hot but the nights are very cold.

These **wild asses** (or donkeys) are related to tame donkeys.

The **addax** has specially wide hooves, to help it walk on sand.

The **sand cat** hunts small desert animals, such as the jerboa.

The **desert hedgehog** eats small animals like insects and scorpions.

Jerboas eat grass and seeds. They can jump high in the air to escape enemies.

WHY DOES this camel look so thin? It has not had anything to eat or drink for days. But as soon as it drinks, it looks fat and well again.

100

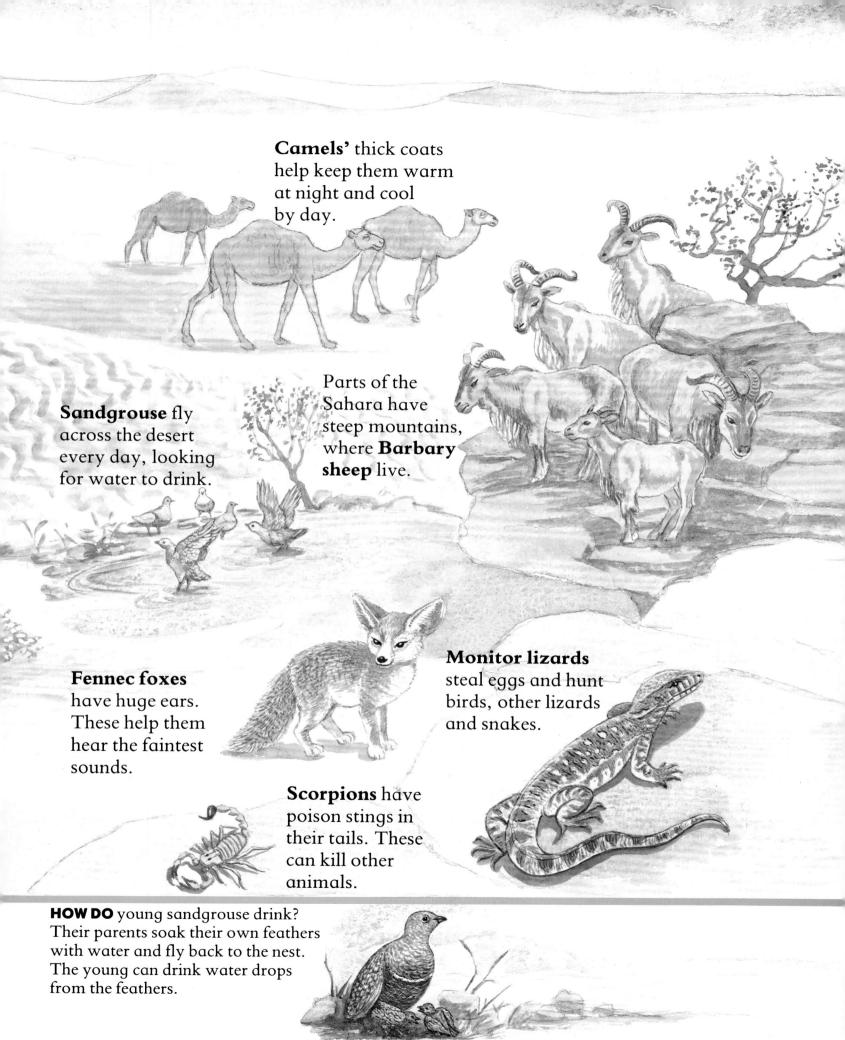

Camels' thick coats help keep them warm at night and cool by day.

Parts of the Sahara have steep mountains, where **Barbary sheep** live.

Sandgrouse fly across the desert every day, looking for water to drink.

Fennec foxes have huge ears. These help them hear the faintest sounds.

Monitor lizards steal eggs and hunt birds, other lizards and snakes.

Scorpions have poison stings in their tails. These can kill other animals.

HOW DO young sandgrouse drink? Their parents soak their own feathers with water and fly back to the nest. The young can drink water drops from the feathers.

ANIMALS IN COLD PLACES

In the far north, it is so cold that no trees will grow. This area is called the tundra. Further south, there are forests, but even here, winters are cold and very long. Only a few kinds of animals can live in these cold places.

Polar bears a[...] good swimmer[...] They hunt oth[...] animals, espec[...]

Walruses live in the icy seas. They eat shellfish from the sea bed.

Arctic hares must watch out for hunters such as foxes and wolves.

Snowy owls hunt by day and night. They catch lemmings and other animals.

Lemmings eat plants. In winter, they make tunnels under the snow.

In summer, **Arctic ground squirrels** store food. They eat it in winter.

WHY DO animals in cold places grow white coats in winter? The hare changes color to help it hide from enemies. The stoat changes color to help it hide while it is hunting.

Arctic hare

winter

summer

Stoat

summer

winter

Reindeer eat moss and other tundra plants. They move south for the winter.

y seals.

Wolves live and hunt in the tundra and northern forests.

Musk oxen have very long hair, to keep them warm in winter.

Arctic foxes have thick coats so they can live in very cold places.

The **lynx** lives in the forests of the very far north.

The **sable** lives in the forests. It has a beautiful coat.

HOW DOES the Arctic fox find food in winter? In summer, when there are more animals to hunt, it hides some of the prey it has killed. It returns to eat it later in the year.

RAINFOREST ANIMALS

Rainforests are amazing places. There are tall trees, thick creepers and hundreds of different kinds of plants and animals. Some of the animals live up in the trees, and others stay in the shadows on the forest floor.

Jaguars are hunters. Their spots make them hard to see in the forest.

Macaws make holes in trees. They build their nests there.

Sloths spend almost all their lives hanging upside down in trees.

The **anaconda** is a huge snake. It lives near water.

WHY DO sloths often look quite green? This is not because they have green coats, but because tiny green plants called algae grow on their fur.

algae on fur

104

Howler monkeys live high in tree-tops. They make very loud noises.

The **emerald tree boa's** green color helps it hide among the leaves.

Marmosets are the world's smallest monkeys.

Young **hoatzin** birds have claws on their wings. They use these for climbing.

Armadillos have hard backs, and huge claws, which they use for digging.

Tapirs live beneath the trees and eat plants that grow near rivers.

Capybaras are like giant guinea pigs. They live in water and on land.

The **toucan's** beak is enormous. It is very light and strong.

WHERE DO the animals live? Some birds and bats live in the tree-tops. Monkeys, sloths and tree frogs live among the branches. Fewer animals live on the forest floor.

Tree-tops

Branches

Forest floor

105

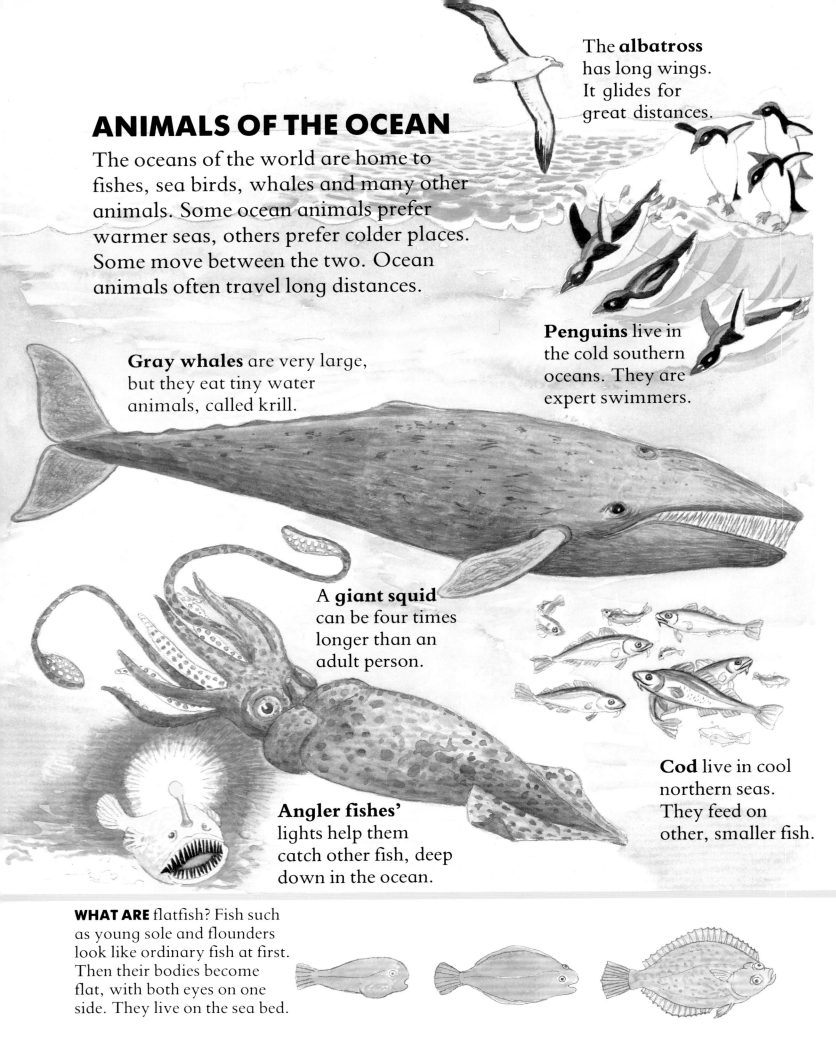

ANIMALS OF THE OCEAN

The oceans of the world are home to fishes, sea birds, whales and many other animals. Some ocean animals prefer warmer seas, others prefer colder places. Some move between the two. Ocean animals often travel long distances.

The **albatross** has long wings. It glides for great distances.

Penguins live in the cold southern oceans. They are expert swimmers.

Gray whales are very large, but they eat tiny water animals, called krill.

A **giant squid** can be four times longer than an adult person.

Cod live in cool northern seas. They feed on other, smaller fish.

Angler fishes' lights help them catch other fish, deep down in the ocean.

WHAT ARE flatfish? Fish such as young sole and flounders look like ordinary fish at first. Then their bodies become flat, with both eyes on one side. They live on the sea bed.

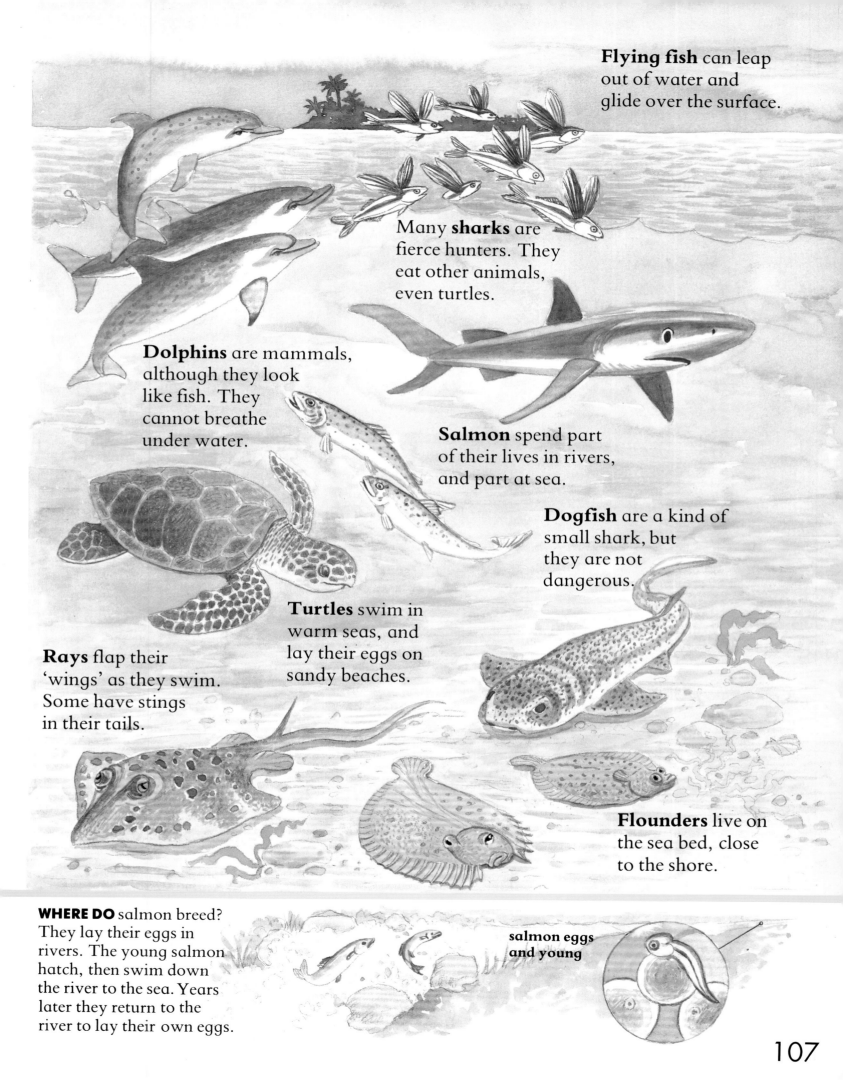

Flying fish can leap out of water and glide over the surface.

Many **sharks** are fierce hunters. They eat other animals, even turtles.

Dolphins are mammals, although they look like fish. They cannot breathe under water.

Salmon spend part of their lives in rivers, and part at sea.

Dogfish are a kind of small shark, but they are not dangerous.

Turtles swim in warm seas, and lay their eggs on sandy beaches.

Rays flap their 'wings' as they swim. Some have stings in their tails.

Flounders live on the sea bed, close to the shore.

WHERE DO salmon breed? They lay their eggs in rivers. The young salmon hatch, then swim down the river to the sea. Years later they return to the river to lay their own eggs.

salmon eggs and young

107

LIFE ON A CORAL REEF

Coral reefs are found in the warm seas of the world. Coral reefs are made up of the skeletons of millions of tiny coral animals. There are many different colors and shapes of coral. Brightly colored fish swim among the corals.

The **lionfish** is beautiful, but it has poison spines on its back.

Giant clams are huge shellfish. They can be three feet across.

The **crown of thorns starfish** eats corals and destroys coral reefs.

The **mandarin fish** hides among the corals and eats smaller fish.

HOW DOES a coral reef grow? Each tiny coral animal grows layers of hard coral underneath itself. Gradually a mound of coral builds up.

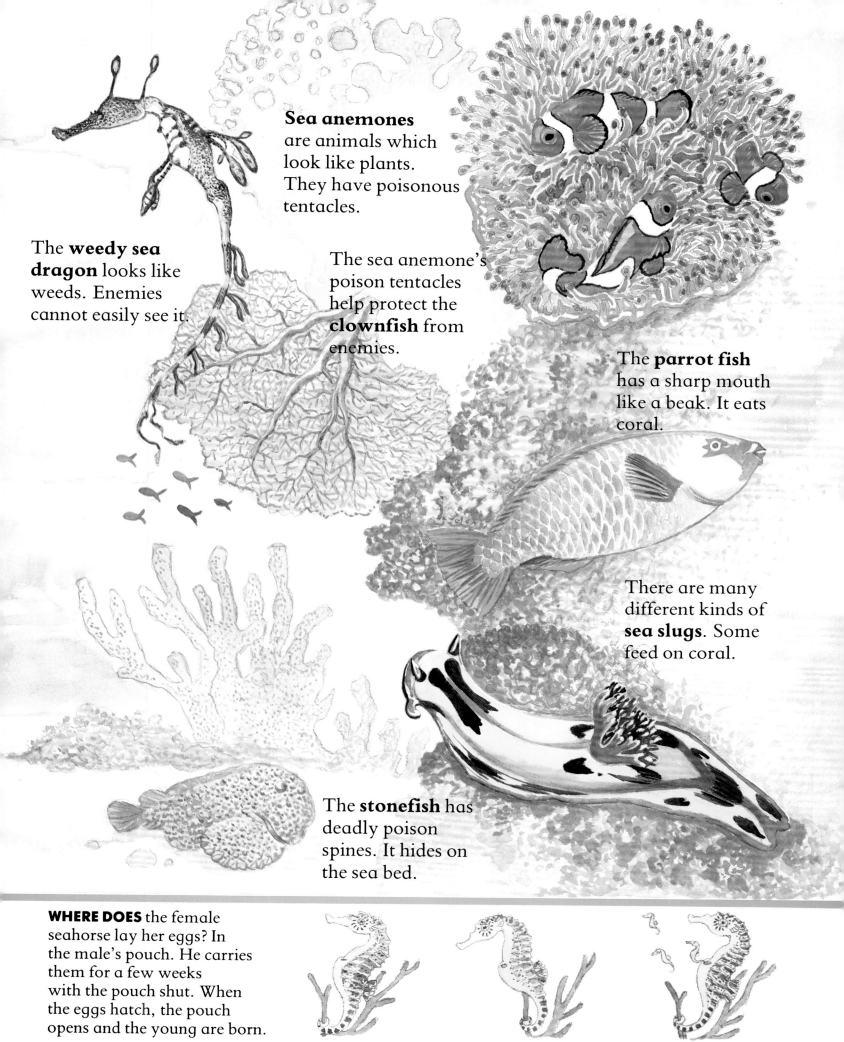

Sea anemones are animals which look like plants. They have poisonous tentacles.

The **weedy sea dragon** looks like weeds. Enemies cannot easily see it.

The sea anemone's poison tentacles help protect the **clownfish** from enemies.

The **parrot fish** has a sharp mouth like a beak. It eats coral.

There are many different kinds of **sea slugs**. Some feed on coral.

The **stonefish** has deadly poison spines. It hides on the sea bed.

WHERE DOES the female seahorse lay her eggs? In the male's pouch. He carries them for a few weeks with the pouch shut. When the eggs hatch, the pouch opens and the young are born.

109

LIFE ON THE SEASHORE

Most seashore animals are small. Some live on rocks. Others bury themselves in sand. Many seashore animals have shells, so they are called shellfish. The birds you see on the seashore are often looking for shellfish and other animals to eat.

Seals catch fish, out at sea. They come ashore to have their pups.

Limpets stick to the rocks. They eat plants that grow there.

Starfish eat shellfish. They use their arms to pull the shellfish open.

Shrimps are tiny, but they catch and eat even tinier animals.

Mussels live together in large groups. They cling on to rocks.

CAN A starfish grow a new arm? Most starfish have five arms. If a starfish loses an arm, it can grow a new one to take its place.

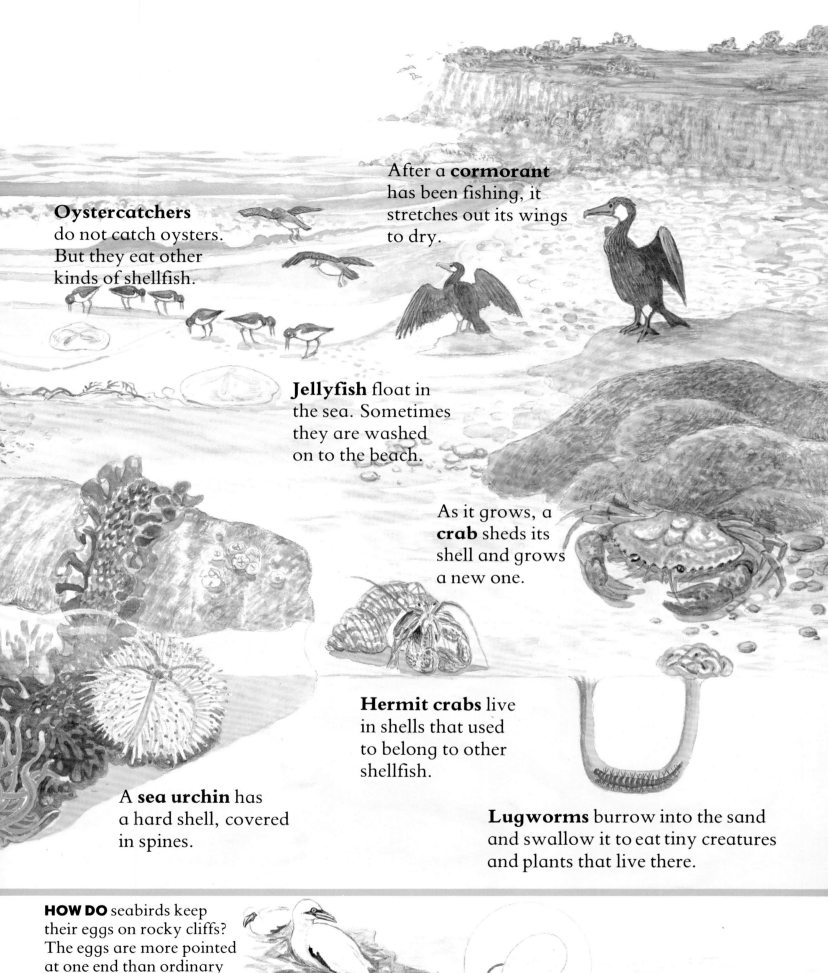

Oystercatchers do not catch oysters. But they eat other kinds of shellfish.

After a **cormorant** has been fishing, it stretches out its wings to dry.

Jellyfish float in the sea. Sometimes they are washed on to the beach.

As it grows, a **crab** sheds its shell and grows a new one.

Hermit crabs live in shells that used to belong to other shellfish.

A **sea urchin** has a hard shell, covered in spines.

Lugworms burrow into the sand and swallow it to eat tiny creatures and plants that live there.

HOW DO seabirds keep their eggs on rocky cliffs? The eggs are more pointed at one end than ordinary eggs. This shape helps stop the eggs from rolling into the sea.

111

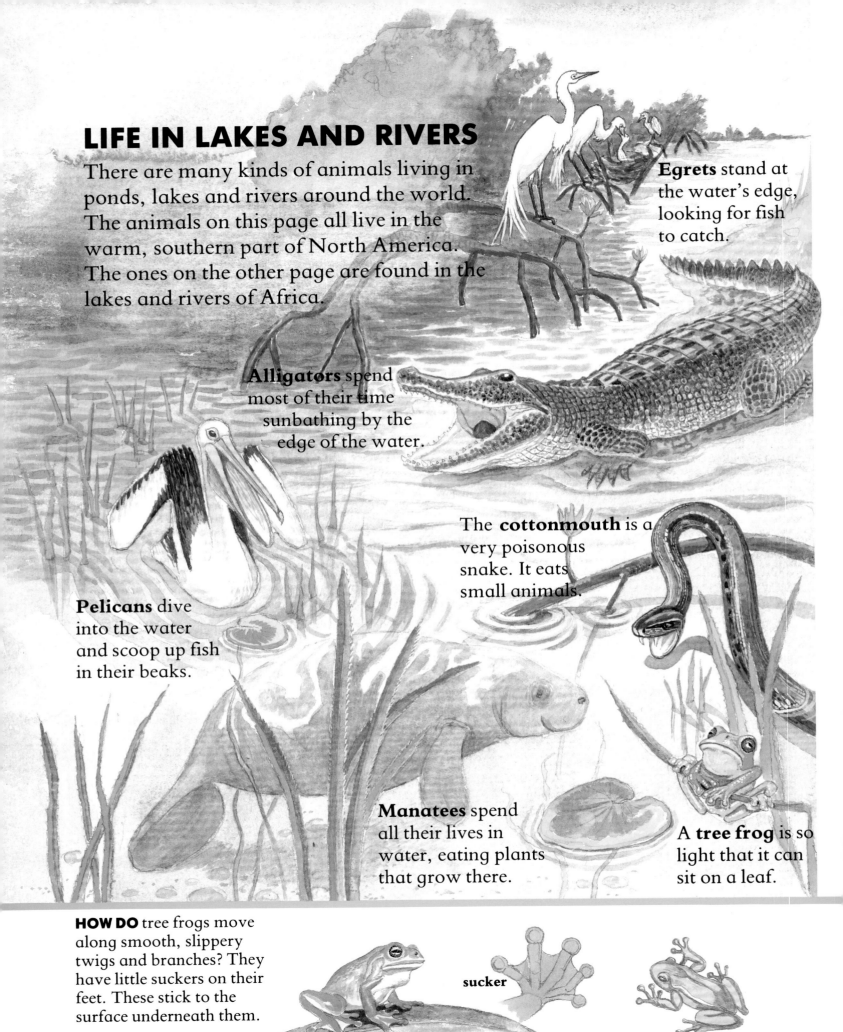

LIFE IN LAKES AND RIVERS

There are many kinds of animals living in ponds, lakes and rivers around the world. The animals on this page all live in the warm, southern part of North America. The ones on the other page are found in the lakes and rivers of Africa.

Egrets stand at the water's edge, looking for fish to catch.

Alligators spend most of their time sunbathing by the edge of the water.

The **cottonmouth** is a very poisonous snake. It eats small animals.

Pelicans dive into the water and scoop up fish in their beaks.

Manatees spend all their lives in water, eating plants that grow there.

A **tree frog** is so light that it can sit on a leaf.

HOW DO tree frogs move along smooth, slippery twigs and branches? They have little suckers on their feet. These stick to the surface underneath them.

sucker

112

Fish eagles are hunters. They eat mice and water birds as well as fish.

Crocodiles catch other animals when they come to the water to drink.

The **Goliath heron** lives by lakes, rivers, and the sea.

The **mouthbrooder** keeps its eggs and its young inside its mouth.

Jacanas are also called 'lily-trotters', because they can walk on water plants.

HOW DO crocodiles find their buried eggs? When the young are hatching, they cry. Their mother hears them and digs up the eggs so the young can get out. Then she carries them to the water, in her mouth.

ANIMALS OF AUSTRALIA

Many Australian plants and animals are different from those in other places. The trees are mostly a kind called eucalyptus. Many animals are 'marsupials'. This means the mother has a pocket in her body, called a pouch. She carries her young in this.

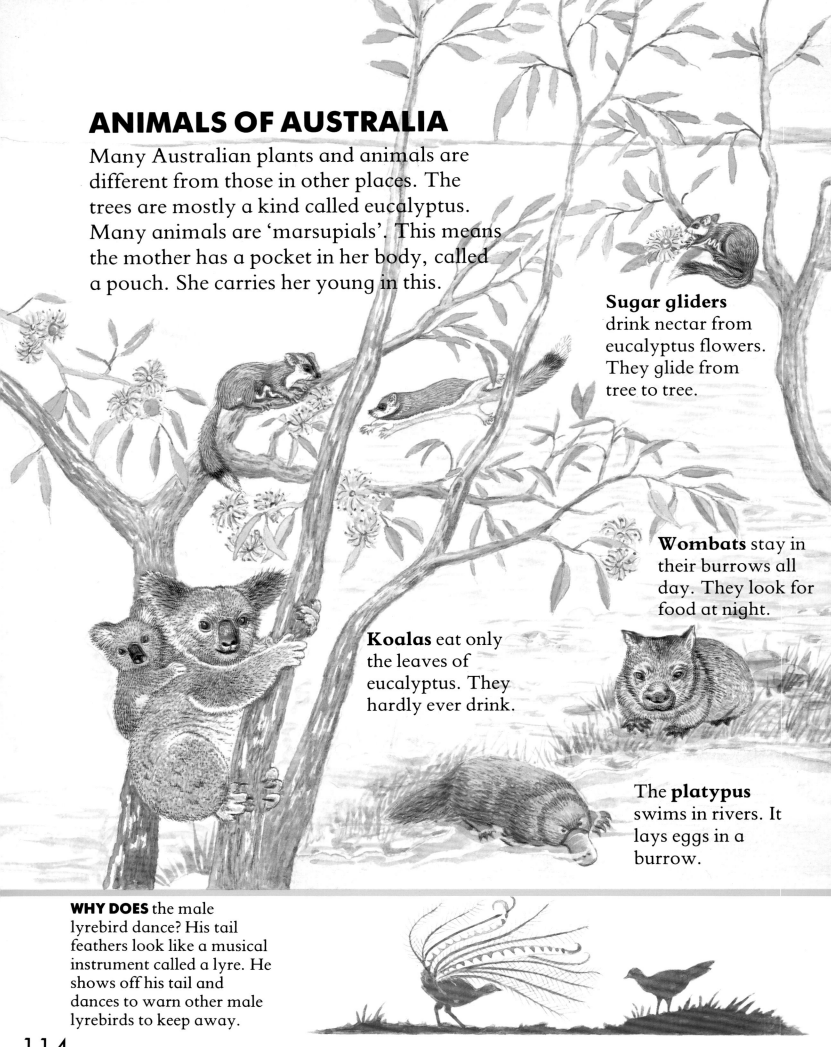

Sugar gliders drink nectar from eucalyptus flowers. They glide from tree to tree.

Wombats stay in their burrows all day. They look for food at night.

Koalas eat only the leaves of eucalyptus. They hardly ever drink.

The **platypus** swims in rivers. It lays eggs in a burrow.

WHY DOES the male lyrebird dance? His tail feathers look like a musical instrument called a lyre. He shows off his tail and dances to warn other male lyrebirds to keep away.

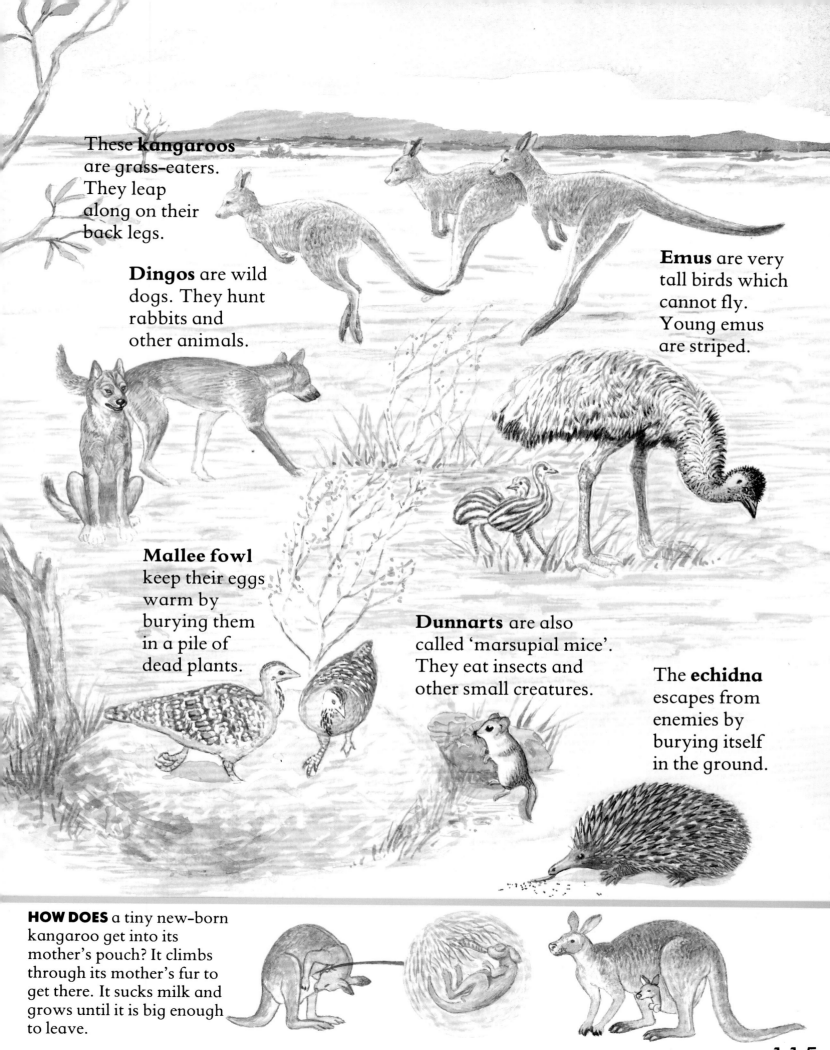

These **kangaroos** are grass-eaters. They leap along on their back legs.

Dingos are wild dogs. They hunt rabbits and other animals.

Emus are very tall birds which cannot fly. Young emus are striped.

Mallee fowl keep their eggs warm by burying them in a pile of dead plants.

Dunnarts are also called 'marsupial mice'. They eat insects and other small creatures.

The **echidna** escapes from enemies by burying itself in the ground.

HOW DOES a tiny new-born kangaroo get into its mother's pouch? It climbs through its mother's fur to get there. It sucks milk and grows until it is big enough to leave.

MINIBEASTS

Many of the animals in the world are quite small ones, without backbones. They are insects, spiders, worms and other creatures that live in the soil. Some fly, and some creep along the ground. One name people sometimes give to all of these different animals is 'minibeasts'.

Mosquitoes bite people and other animals. They drink their blood.

Centipedes have poisonous claws. They kill and eat other small animals.

Millipedes eat plants. Most are small. This giant one lives in Africa.

Earthworms eat dead plants. They drag these underground into their burrows.

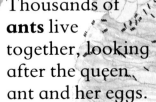

Dragonflies lay their eggs in water. You can see dragonflies near streams.

Thousands of **ants** live together, looking after the queen ant and her eggs.

HOW DO butterflies grow?

They lay eggs on leaves. Caterpillars hatch.

They eat leaves and grow.

Each caterpillar becomes a chrysalis.

Inside this it becomes a butterfly.

It comes out.

It dries its wings and flies away.

116

The **garden spider** builds a web to trap insects.

Ladybirds are useful. They eat little insects called aphids, which damage plants.

The **garden snail** lives in cool, damp places. It eats plants.

Fireflies are beetles that glow in the dark. They live in hot countries.

Monarch butterflies live in North America. They fly south every winter.

Bees make honey, to feed their young. People keep bees in hives.

HOW DOES a spider make a web?

It starts with one strand.

Then it makes more strands like the spokes of a wheel.

It weaves around the spokes.

117

AMAZING ANIMALS

This picture shows some unusual animals. Some are enormous. Others can run very fast, or travel long distances. Some have unusual ways of catching prey, or hiding from the enemies. Others just look rather strange or colorful.

There are many kinds of **birds of paradise**. The males have very beautiful feathers.

Komodo dragons are the biggest lizards of all. They can be nine feet long.

Blue whales are the biggest animals that have ever lived. They can be 90 feet long.

Elephant seals are the biggest of all seals. They have trunks that look a bit like an elephant's.

Mudskippers are fish which crawl out of water on to tree roots.

HOW DO mudskippers stay out of the water? They take in air through their skins, but they cannot stay out of water for very long.

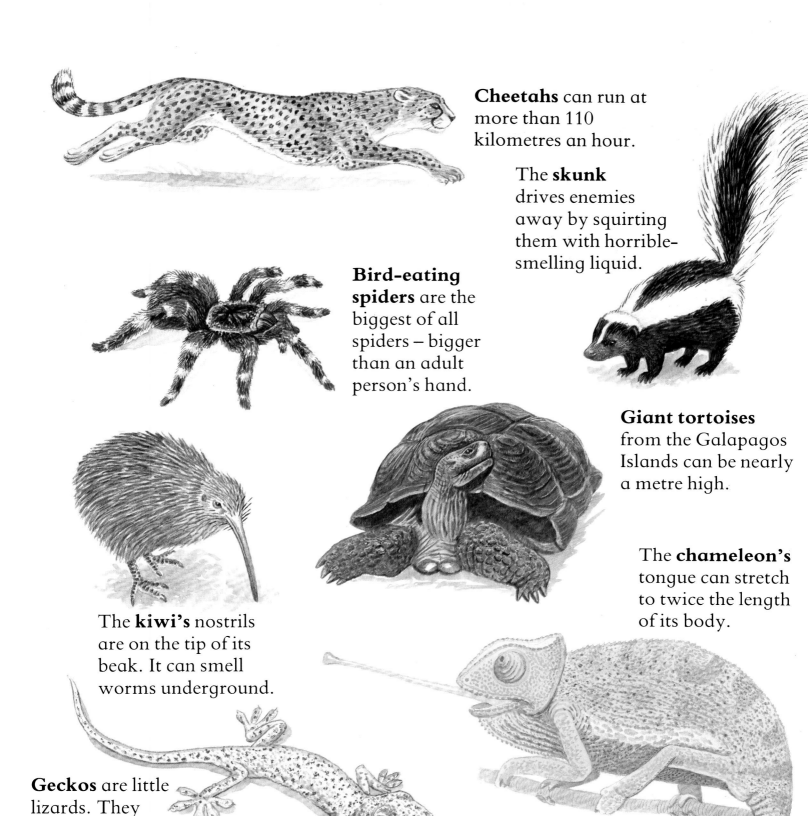

Cheetahs can run at more than 110 kilometres an hour.

The **skunk** drives enemies away by squirting them with horrible-smelling liquid.

Bird-eating spiders are the biggest of all spiders – bigger than an adult person's hand.

Giant tortoises from the Galapagos Islands can be nearly a metre high.

The **chameleon's** tongue can stretch to twice the length of its body.

The **kiwi's** nostrils are on the tip of its beak. It can smell worms underground.

Geckos are little lizards. They can walk upside down on the ceiling.

CAN A chameleon change colour? It cannot change completely, but it can become darker to match dark surroundings. If it is annoyed, it can turn nearly black.

119

ANIMALS IN DANGER

All over the world, there are animals in danger of dying out. People hunt and kill them, for meat or for fur. Sometimes people use the land where the animals live, and there is nowhere for the animals to go. Pollution is also very harmful to wildlife.

Ospreys eat fish. Pollution in the water harms the fish and the ospreys.

People have killed many **tigers** for their skins. Now they are rare.

Turtles lay their eggs on beaches. But people sometimes dig the eggs up.

Monk seals live in the Mediterranean sea. Pollution there harms the seals.

People cut down the forests where **orangutans** live.

HOW CAN animals be saved? Saiga antelopes on the grasslands of Asia were also hunted. When the hunting was stopped their numbers grew from a few hundred fifty years ago, to more than two million today.

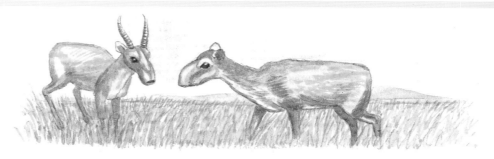

120

Giant otters live in Brazil. They are the rarest of all otters.

Gorillas live in African forests. Many are killed by hunters.

Kakapos are parrots from New Zealand. They cannot fly, so cats catch them.

Hunters have shot so many **Siberian white cranes** that there are very few left.

Pandas eat bamboo. In some places, this is dying, so the pandas have no food.

People kill **rhinoceroses** to get their horns. This is not allowed, but it still happens.

WHY DID the dodo die out? This large bird, from the island of Mauritius, could not fly. Sailors visiting the island killed so many dodos that there were none left at all.

ANIMALS OF LONG AGO

The animals in this picture all lived on earth millions of years ago. They did not all live at the same time. Some of them are dinosaurs. The last of the dinosaurs died over 65 million years ago, but some had gone long before that.

This dinosaur belonged to a group called **hadrosaurs.** They had odd-shaped heads.

Tyrannosaurus was a hunter, which killed and ate other dinosaurs.

Ichthyosaurs were swimming reptiles. They had sharp teeth for catching fish.

Diatryma was a bird which did not fly. It was six feet tall.

Plesiosaurus was a reptile which swam in the sea and ate fish.

Iguanodon had front feet like hands and long back legs for running.

HOW LONG ago did these animals live?

Stegosaurus lived about 150 million years ago

Iguanodon lived about 120 million years ago

Ichthyosaurs lived about 200 million years ago

Triceratops' horns made it look fierce, but it ate only plants.

Brachiosaurus was one of the biggest animals that ever lived.

Hyracotherium was the first kind of horse. It was only about one foot tall.

Pterosaurs were flying reptiles. Some kinds were huge, and others were small.

Stegosaurus had spikes on its tail to protect it from meat-eating dinosaurs.

Dromiceiomimus had big eyes and a beak. It could run very fast.

Tyrannosaurus lived about 70 million years ago

Diatryma lived about 50 million years ago

People like us have been on the earth for about 100,000 years

INDEX

INDEX

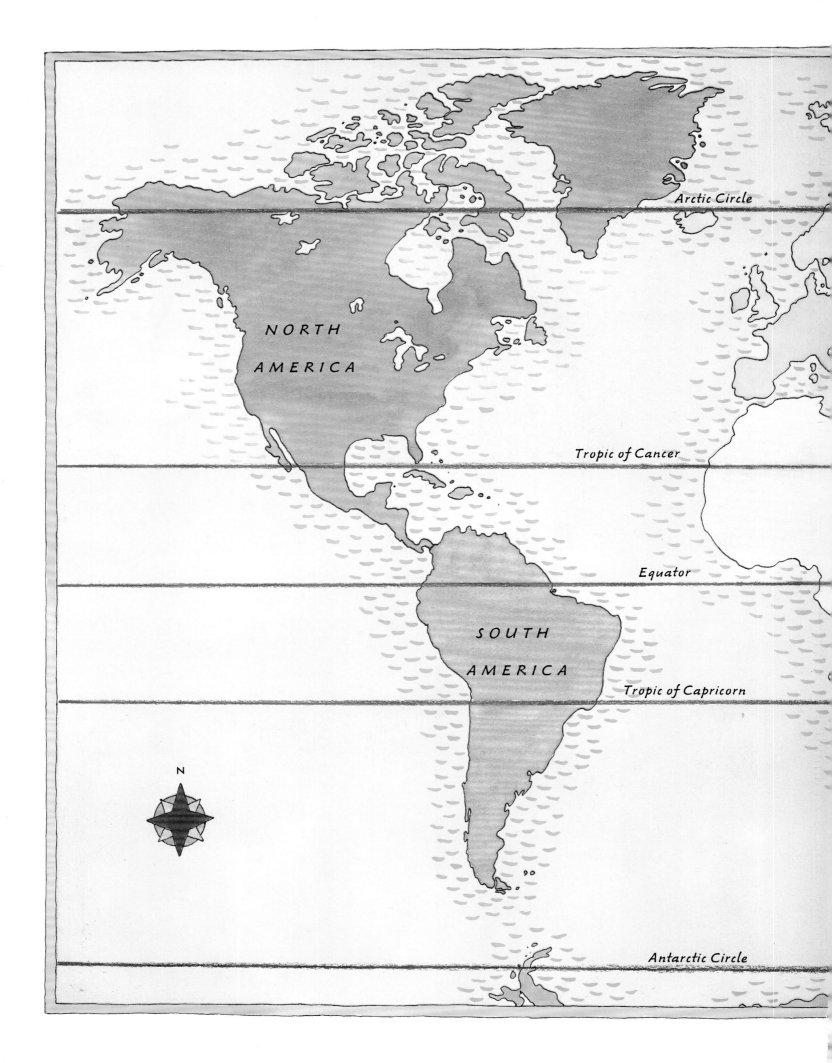

Arctic Circle

NORTH

AMERICA

Tropic of Cancer

Equator

N

SOUTH

AMERICA

Tropic of Capricorn

Antarctic Circle